Folk Toys

0 11557 02920 8

Folk Toys

Patterns & Projects for the Scroll Saw

Ken Folk

STACKPOLE
BOOKS

Contents

Introduction
6

The Projects

Sources of Supply
77
Metric Conversions
78

Introduction

One surefire way to put smiles on children's faces is to give them amusing toys with moving parts. Early American toymakers realized this and went to great lengths to provide plenty of eye-catching antics with animation.

Early toys were crude and scarce because the colonists' lives consisted of long hours of labor with little time or money for amusement for themselves or their children. The Industrial Revolution, however, brought increased prosperity and leisure time to Americans, and toymaking developed. By the second half of the nineteenth century, hinges, cranks, and mechanical devices became common features on wooden folk toys. Soon, ingenious toy manufacturers built on these ideas as well as on techniques for clockworks passed down from their European fathers, and a multimillion-dollar industry was at hand.

The world has changed since that time. Plastic and video dominate the market. But these clever toys still offer timeless appeal for home craftsmen and their children. This book offers a collection of patterns for animated classics that were popular during the late-nineteenth and early-twentieth centuries as well as some of my own designs. You'll find a woman with a moving staff herding a flock of waddling geese, birds with nodding heads and flapping wings, animals that scuttle across the floor, and a beetle with feelers that swing from side to side. The toys are operated with pull cords, cranks, hand motions, or simple gravity.

PLANNING THE PROJECT

All of the projects in this book contain full-size patterns. My favorite method for transferring the shape of each part onto the wood is to use cardboard patterns that can be moved around for best position and then traced. Start by photocopying the patterns from the book. Then glue the copies onto a thin sheet (about 1/64-inch thick) of poster board. It can be easily cut with scissors, but it's stiff enough to trace. I buy the 22-by-38-inch size for less than $1 at arts-and-crafts or stationary stores.

If you are a novice scroll sawer and need more information on techniques, consult John Nelson's *Patterns and Projects for the Scroll Saw*, published by Stackpole Books.

MATERIALS

Most of the toys in this book require about one square foot of wood, so cost is not a significant part of the project. Pick a wood that is strong, resists splintering, and finishes well. Hard maple has these qualities in addition to a very tight grain, which makes it easy to get a glass-smooth finish with paint or varnish. You'll find that cutting and sanding hard maple is slow going, but the improved appearance and life of the toy make it worth the extra effort.

ASSEMBLY AND FINISHING

Before assembly, make sure that the parts have been smoothly sanded and that all corners and edges have been rounded to at least a $1/32$-inch radius to prevent splintering. Then temporarily assemble the toy without glue to make sure that there is a loose fit between the moving parts. When you're satisfied with the fit, disassemble the toy and apply the finish to each part except for glued surfaces, pivot joints, and wheel axles.

There are many alternatives for finishing your toys, but whatever you choose, it must be nontoxic. For painted surfaces, I prefer an oil-base primer and topcoat for durability and a sprayed-on lacquer finish for the clear parts.

The last step is to apply the facial, body, and ornamental details. There are two ways to do this type of decorating: hand painting and sign film. For hand painting, make a full-size photocopy of the decoration, transfer it onto the project with carbon paper, and then paint in the details. The sign film technique is an excellent alternative for those who don't want to attempt hand painting. Sign film is made in dozens of colors and is sold by the foot at art supply stores. The film is about as thick as a human hair, so that when applied it's difficult to tell the difference from paint. To begin, transfer the decoration on to the sign film using a photocopy and carbon paper. Cut out the detail with a scissors or craft knife. Peel off the paper backing and apply it to the project. If it doesn't look right, remove it and try again.

To ensure that the toy runs smoothly, rub some candle wax on the wearing surfaces of the axles, pivots, and rubbing parts for lubrication. To finish, assemble the toy with a quality yellow glue or epoxy.

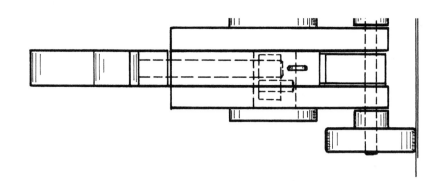

SHOREBIRD

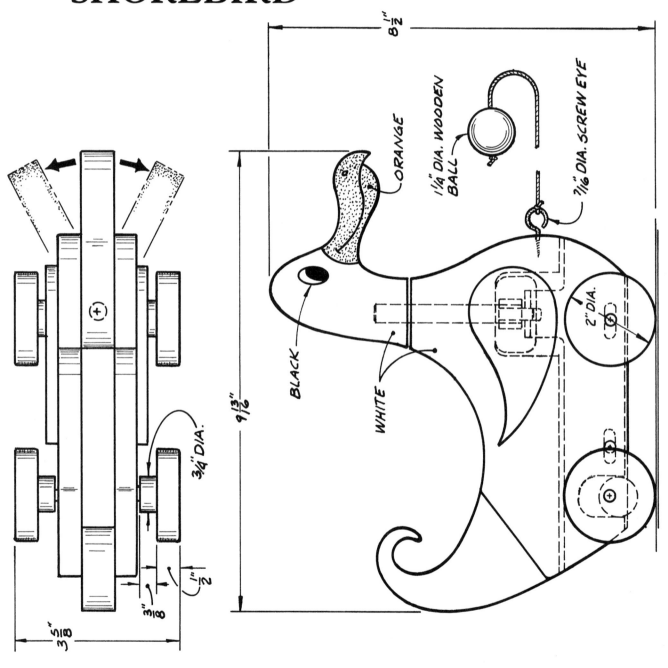

$8\frac{1}{2}"$

ORANGE

$\frac{1}{4}"$ DIA. WOODEN BALL

$\frac{7}{16}"$ DIA. SCREW EYE

BLACK

WHITE

2" DIA.

$9\frac{13}{16}"$

$\frac{3}{4}"$ DIA.

$\frac{1}{2}"$

$\frac{3}{8}"$

$3\frac{5}{8}"$

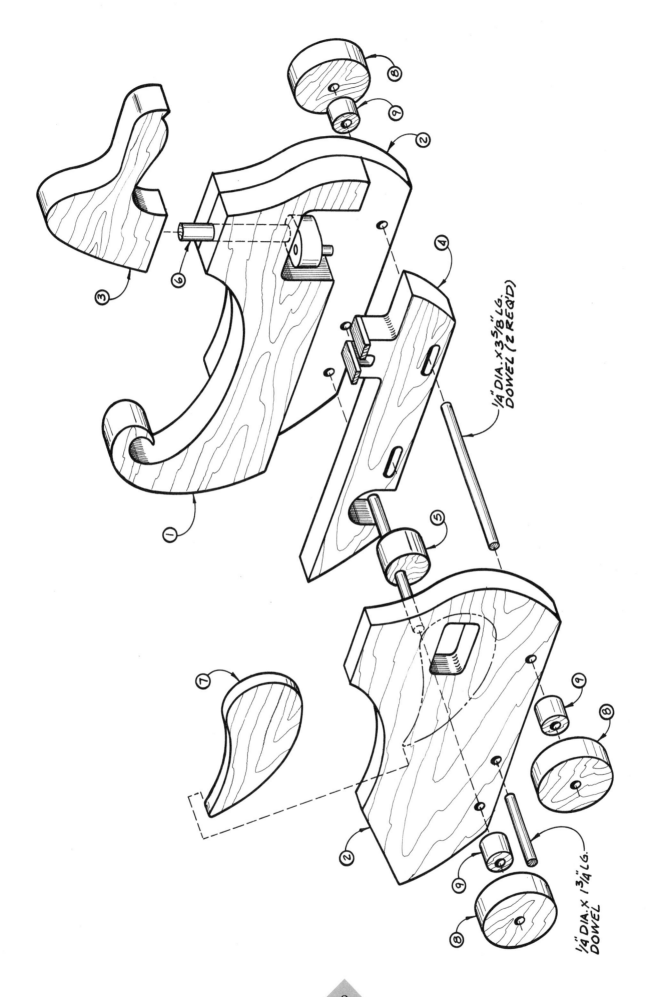

¼" DIA. X 3⅝" LG.
DOWEL (2 REQ'D)

¼" DIA. X 1¾" LG.
DOWEL

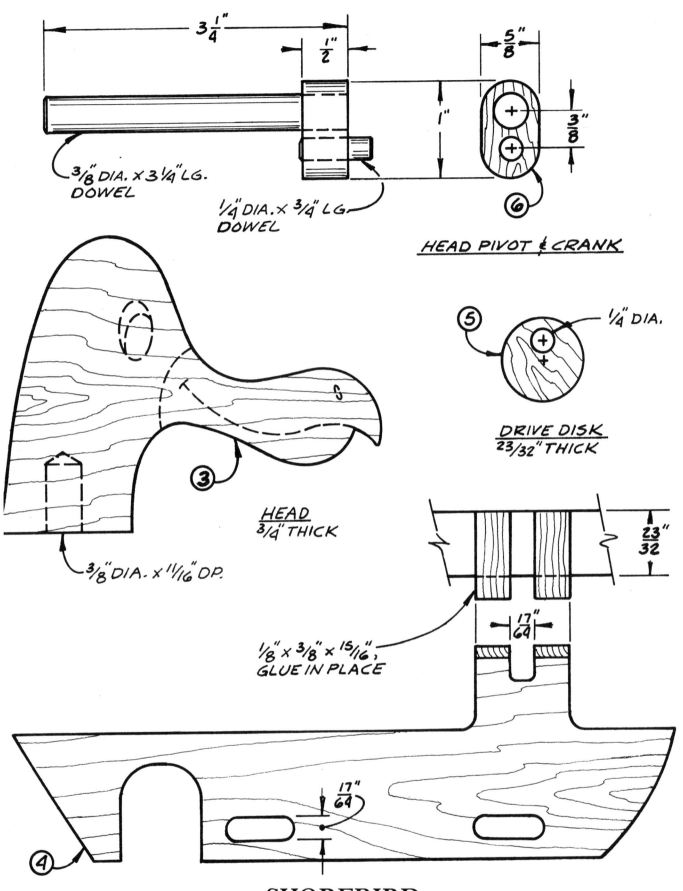

$3\frac{1}{4}$"

$\frac{1}{2}$"

$\frac{5}{8}$"

1"

$\frac{3}{8}$"

$\frac{3}{8}$" DIA. X $3\frac{1}{4}$" LG.
DOWEL

$\frac{1}{4}$" DIA. X $\frac{3}{4}$" LG.
DOWEL

6

HEAD PIVOT & CRANK

5

$\frac{1}{4}$" DIA.

DRIVE DISK
23/32" THICK

$\frac{3}{8}$" DIA. X $1\frac{1}{16}$" DP.

3

HEAD
$\frac{3}{4}$" THICK

$\frac{23}{32}$"

$\frac{17}{64}$"

$\frac{1}{8}$" X $\frac{3}{8}$" X $\frac{15}{16}$",
GLUE IN PLACE

$\frac{17}{64}$"

4

SHOREBIRD
FULL-SIZE PATTERNS

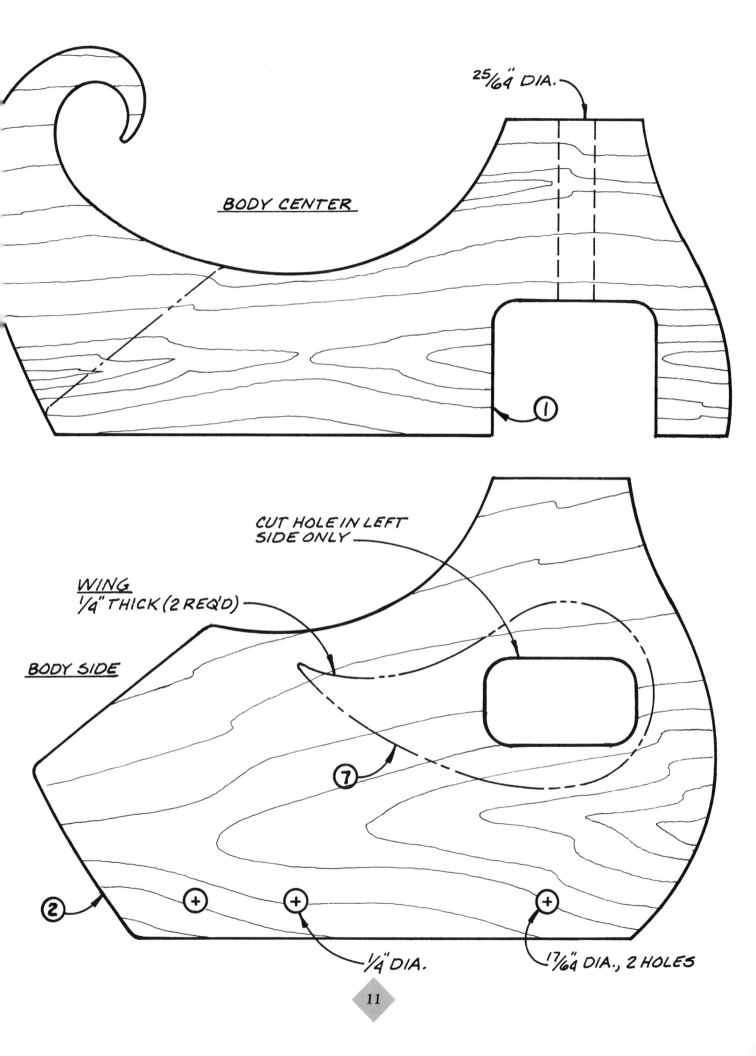

25/64" DIA.

BODY CENTER

①

WING
1/4" THICK (2 REQ'D)

CUT HOLE IN LEFT
SIDE ONLY

BODY SIDE

②

⑦

1/4" DIA.

17/64" DIA., 2 HOLES

11

LUMBERJACKS

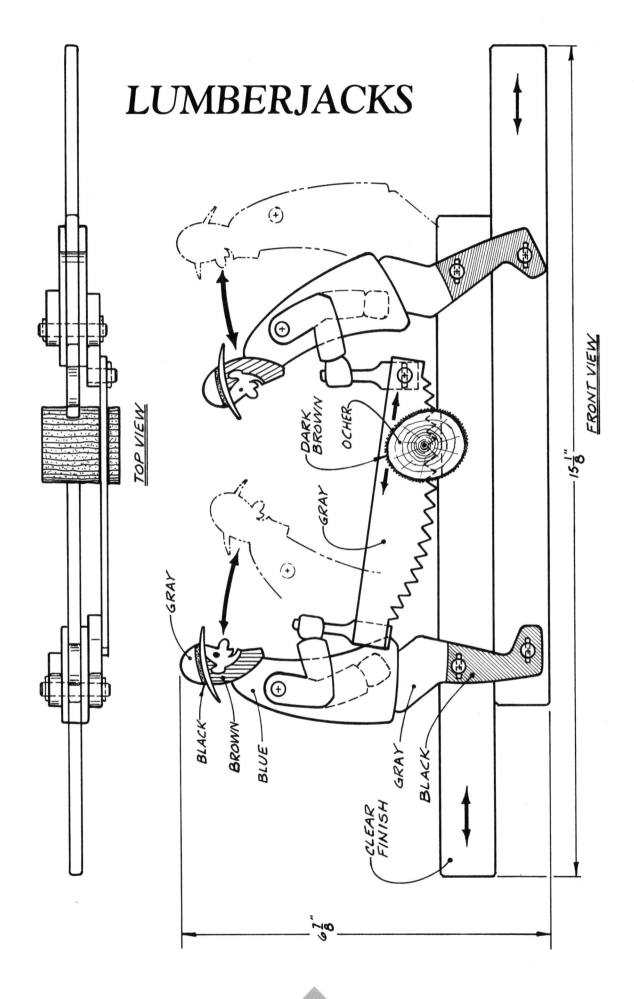

TOP VIEW

FRONT VIEW

15⅛"

6⅞"

GRAY

DARK BROWN

OCHER

GRAY

GRAY

BLACK

BROWN

BLUE

CLEAR FINISH

GRAY

BLACK

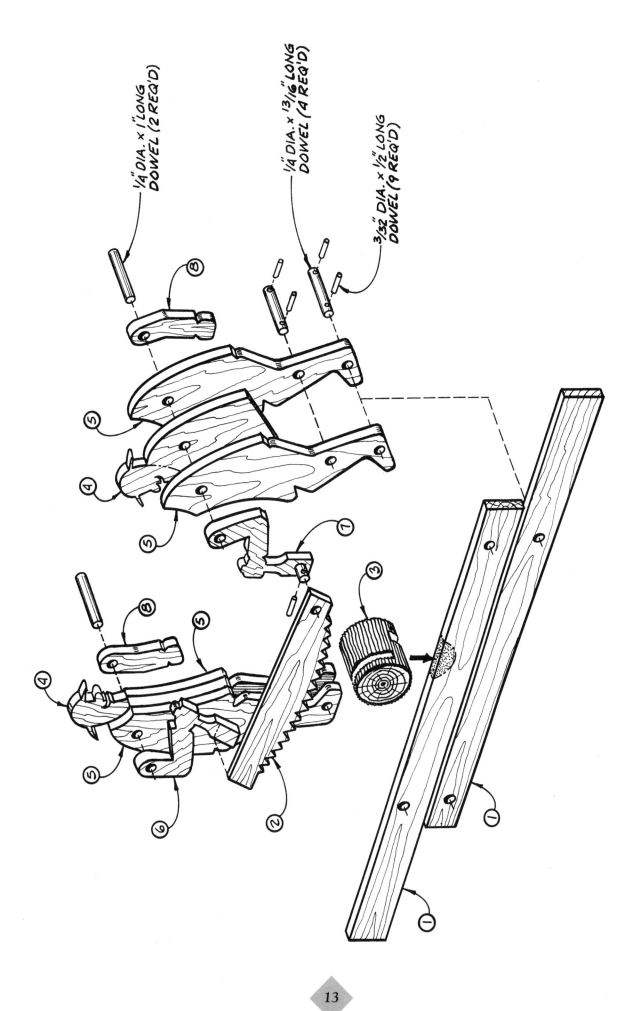

1/4" DIA. x 1" LONG DOWEL (2 REQ'D)

1/4" DIA. x 13/16" LONG DOWEL (4 REQ'D)

3/32" DIA. x 1/2" LONG DOWEL (9 REQ'D)

8

5

4

5

7

8

5

4

5

6

2

3

1

1

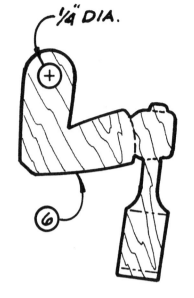

¼" DIA.

ARM
¼" THICK (2 REQ'D)

⑥

GROOVE WITH
A VEINING CHISEL

$\frac{3}{16}$"

③

$\frac{1}{4}$"

LOG

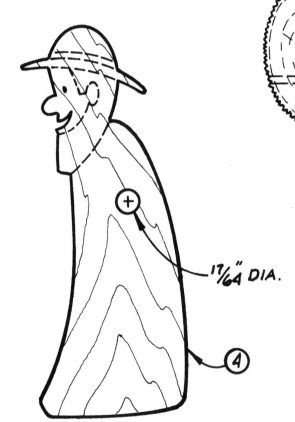

1$\frac{7}{64}$" DIA.

④

BODY CENTER
¼" THICK (2 REQ'D)

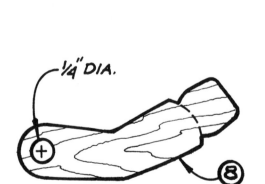

¼" DIA.

⑧

ARM
¼" THICK (2 REQ'D)

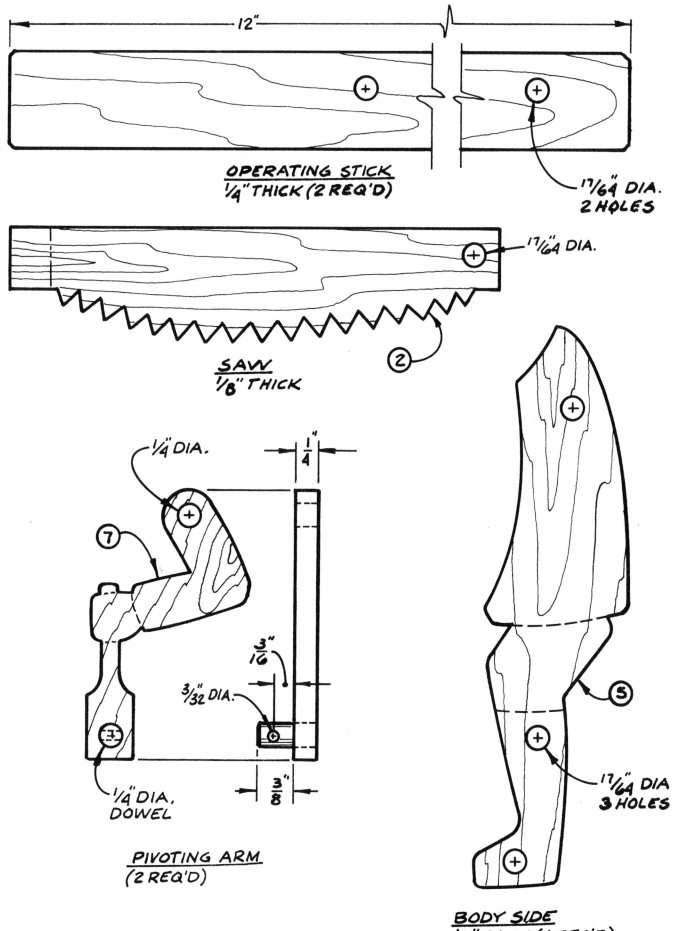

12"

OPERATING STICK
1/4" THICK (2 REQ'D)

17/64" DIA.
2 HOLES

17/64" DIA.

SAW
1/8" THICK

2

1/4 DIA.

1/4

7

3/16"

3/32" DIA.

3/8"

1/4" DIA.
DOWEL

PIVOTING ARM
(2 REQ'D)

5

17/64" DIA
3 HOLES

BODY SIDE
1/8" THICK (4 REQ'D)

15

LADIES CHURNING BUTTER

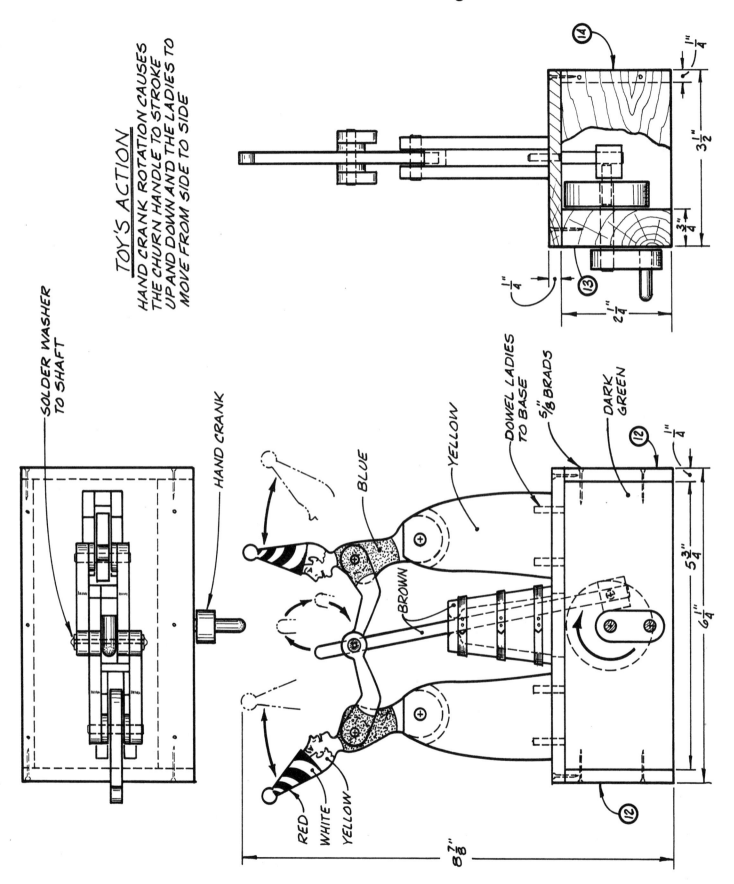

TOY'S ACTION
HAND CRANK ROTATION CAUSES
THE CHURN HANDLE TO STROKE
UP AND DOWN AND THE LADIES TO
MOVE FROM SIDE TO SIDE

SOLDER WASHER
TO SHAFT

HAND CRANK

BLUE

YELLOW

DOWEL LADIES
TO BASE

5/8" BRADS

DARK
GREEN

BROWN

RED
WHITE
YELLOW

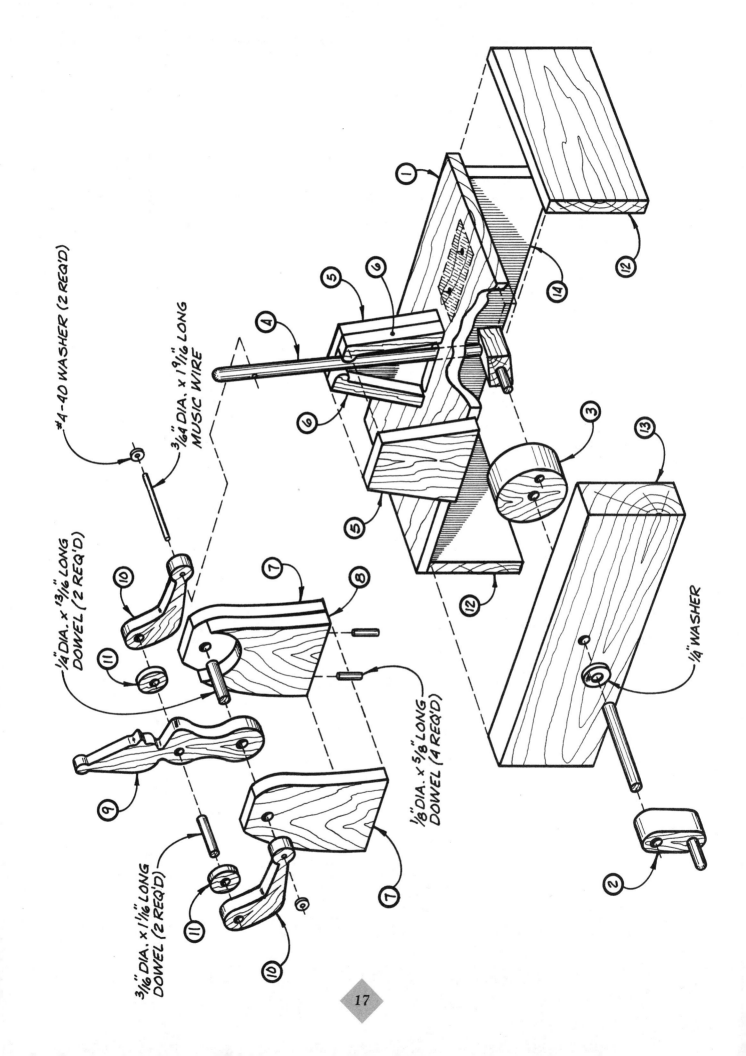

#4-40 WASHER (2 REQ'D)

3/64" DIA. x 19/16" LONG
MUSIC WIRE

1/4" DIA. x 13/16" LONG
DOWEL (2 REQ'D)

3/16" DIA. x 1 1/16" LONG
DOWEL (2 REQ'D)

1/8" DIA. x 5/8" LONG
DOWEL (4 REQ'D)

1/4" WASHER

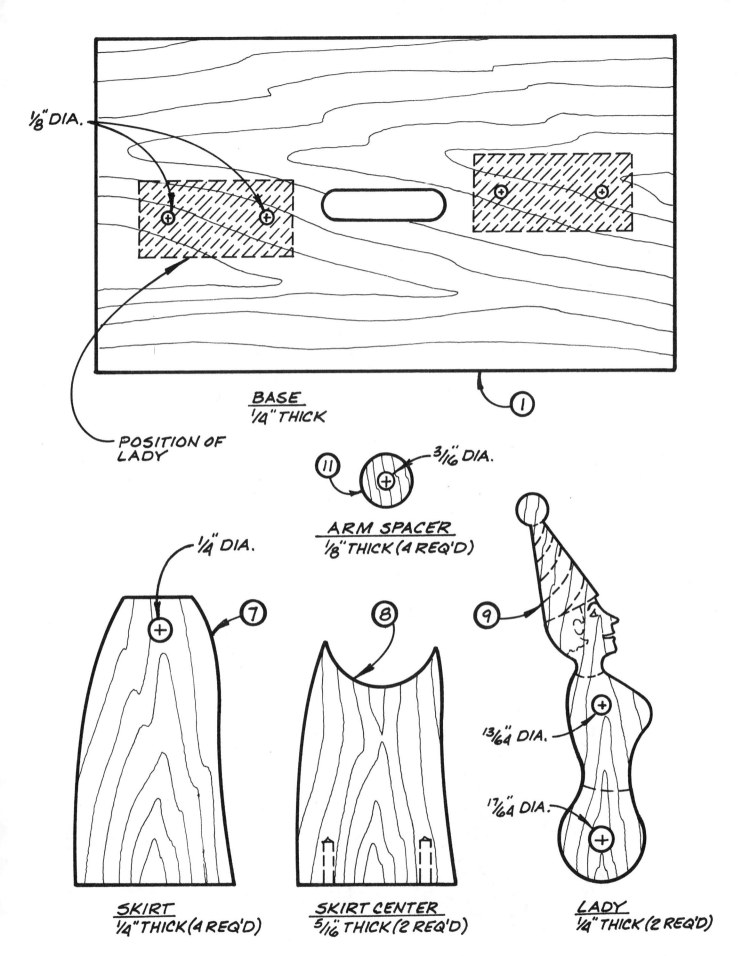

⅛" DIA.

POSITION OF LADY

BASE
¼" THICK

①

11 3/16" DIA.

ARM SPACER
⅛" THICK (4 REQ'D)

¼" DIA.

⑦

⑧

⑨

13/64" DIA.

17/64" DIA.

SKIRT
¼" THICK (4 REQ'D)

SKIRT CENTER
5/16" THICK (2 REQ'D)

LADY
¼" THICK (2 REQ'D)

LADIES CHURNING BUTTER
FULL-SIZE PATTERNS

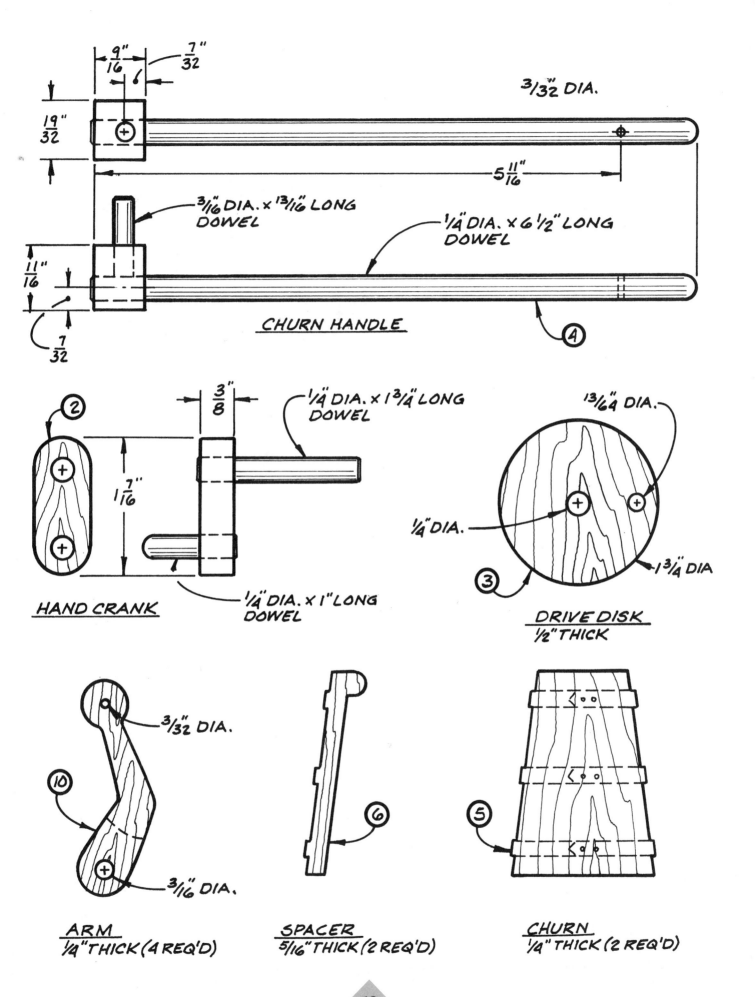

$\frac{9}{16}$"

$\frac{7}{32}$"

$\frac{19}{32}$"

$\frac{3}{32}$" DIA.

$5\frac{11}{16}$"

$\frac{3}{16}$" DIA. x $1\frac{3}{16}$" LONG DOWEL

$\frac{1}{4}$" DIA. x $6\frac{1}{2}$" LONG DOWEL

$\frac{11}{16}$"

$\frac{7}{32}$"

CHURN HANDLE

④

$\frac{3}{8}$"

$1\frac{7}{16}$"

$\frac{1}{4}$" DIA. x $1\frac{3}{4}$" LONG DOWEL

②

$\frac{1}{4}$" DIA. x 1" LONG DOWEL

HAND CRANK

$\frac{13}{64}$" DIA.

$\frac{1}{4}$" DIA.

$1\frac{3}{4}$" DIA

③

DRIVE DISK
$\frac{1}{2}$" THICK

$\frac{3}{32}$" DIA.

⑩

$\frac{3}{16}$" DIA.

ARM
$\frac{1}{4}$" THICK (4 REQ'D)

⑥

SPACER
$\frac{5}{16}$" THICK (2 REQ'D)

⑤

CHURN
$\frac{1}{4}$" THICK (2 REQ'D)

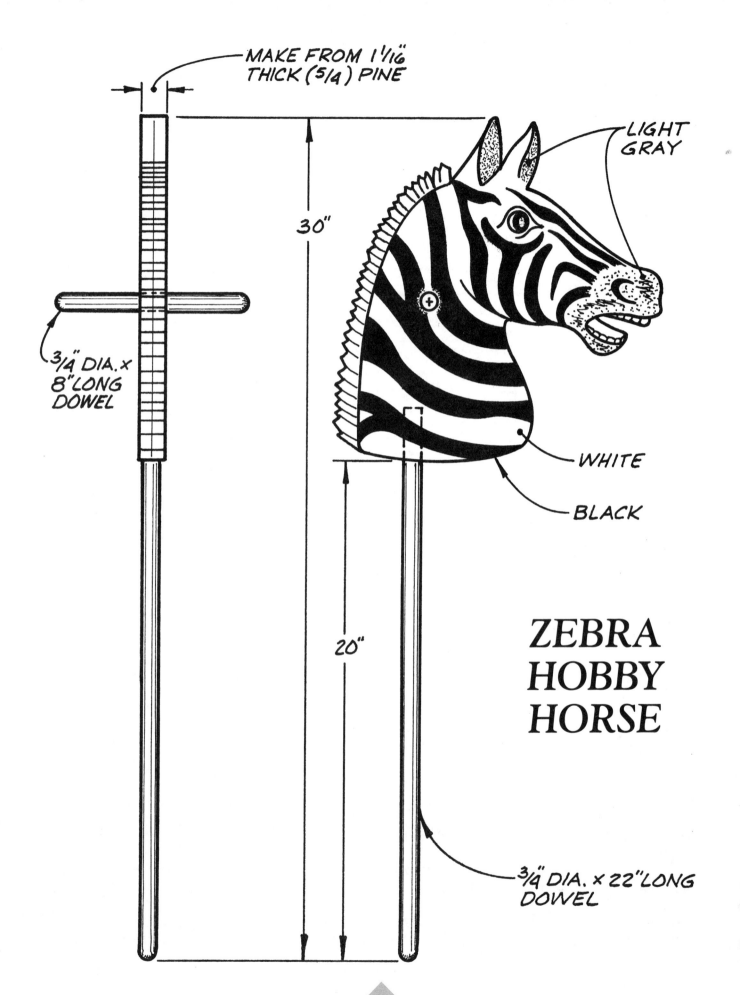

MAKE FROM 1¹/₁₆"
THICK (5/4) PINE

30"

LIGHT
GRAY

¾" DIA. x
8" LONG
DOWEL

WHITE

BLACK

ZEBRA
HOBBY
HORSE

20"

¾" DIA. x 22" LONG
DOWEL

20

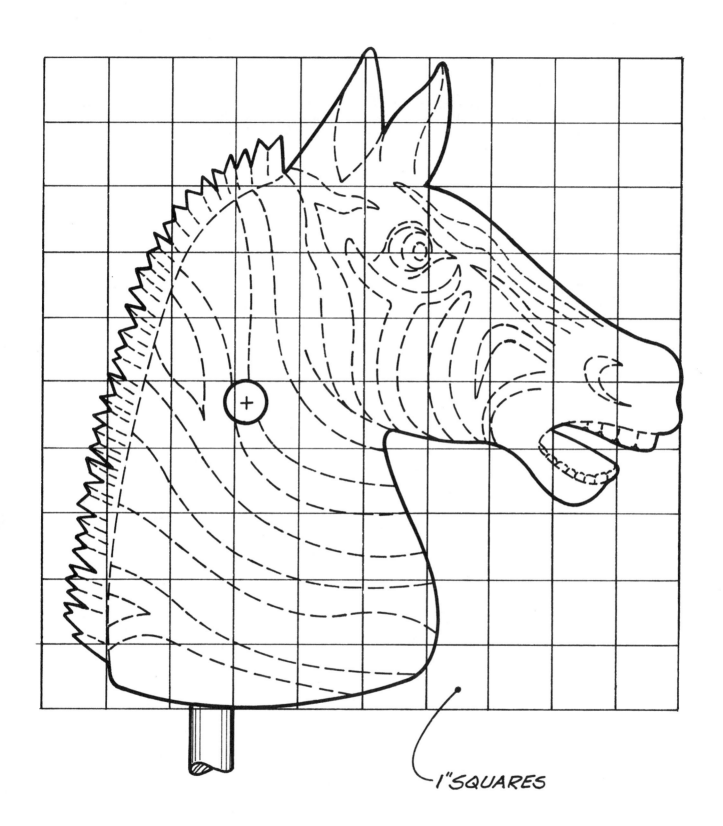

1"SQUARES

FULL-SIZE PATTERN

HORSE WITH MOVING RIDER

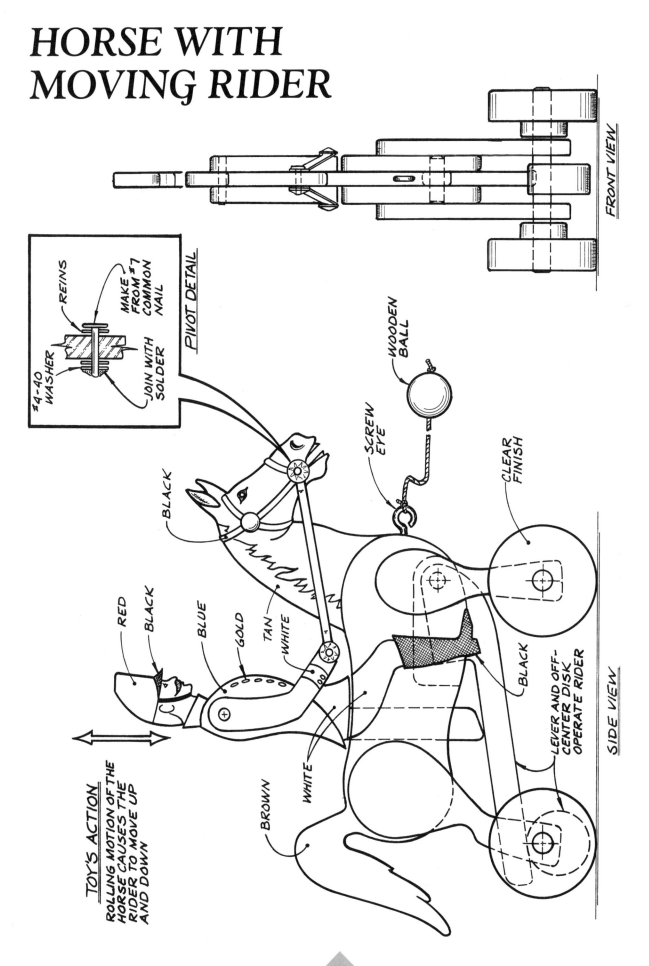

FRONT VIEW

PIVOT DETAIL

REINS

#4-40 WASHER

JOIN WITH SOLDER

MAKE FROM #7 COMMON NAIL

WOODEN BALL

SCREW EYE

CLEAR FINISH

BLACK

RED

BLACK

BLUE

GOLD

TAN

WHITE

BROWN

WHITE

BLACK

LEVER AND OFF-CENTER DISK OPERATE RIDER

SIDE VIEW

TOY'S ACTION
ROLLING MOTION OF THE HORSE CAUSES THE RIDER TO MOVE UP AND DOWN

22

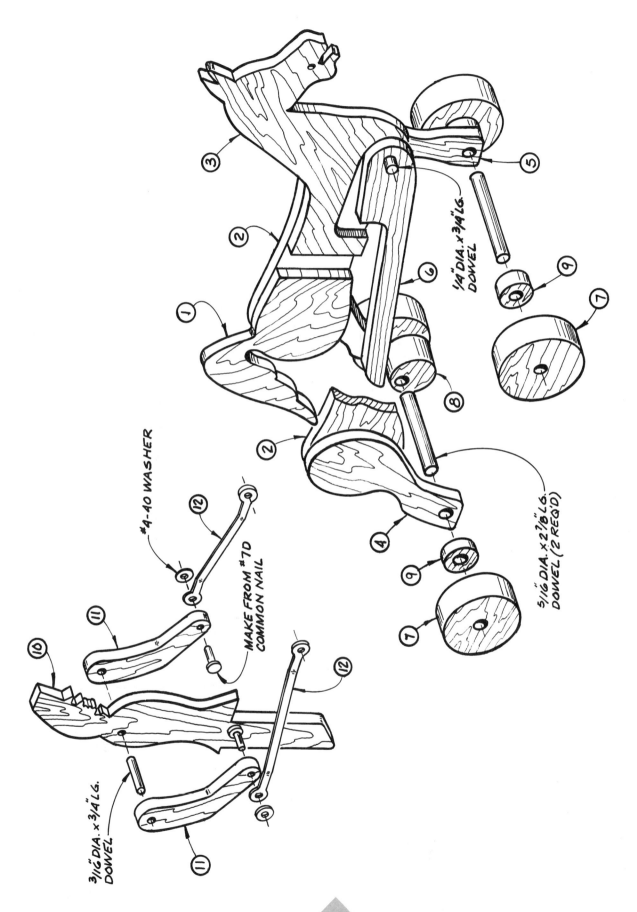

3

2

1

5

¼" DIA. x ¾" LG.
DOWEL

9

6

7

8

9

7

5/16" DIA. x 2⅞" LG.
DOWEL (2 REQ'D)

2

4

#4-40 WASHER

12

MAKE FROM #7D
COMMON NAIL

11

10

12

3/16" DIA. x ¾" LG.
DOWEL

11

HORSE WITH MOVING RIDER

FULL-SIZE
PATTERNS

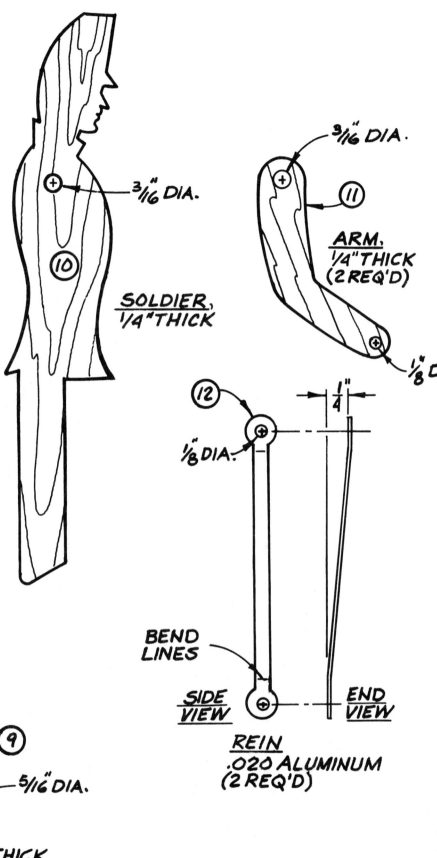

SOLDIER,
1/4" THICK

3/16" DIA.

10

3/16" DIA.

11

ARM,
1/4" THICK
(2 REQ'D)

1/8" DIA

12

1/8" DIA.

1/4"

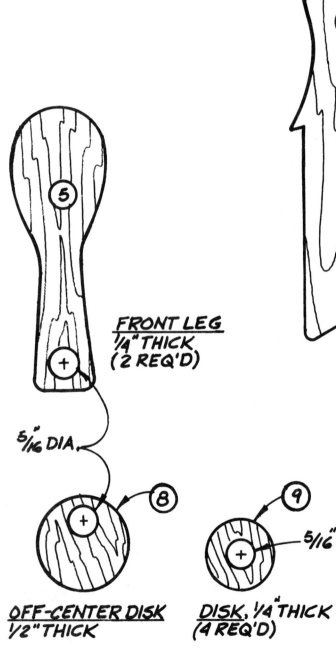

5

FRONT LEG
1/4" THICK
(2 REQ'D)

5/16" DIA.

8

9

5/16" DIA.

OFF-CENTER DISK
1/2" THICK

DISK, 1/4" THICK
(4 REQ'D)

BEND
LINES

SIDE
VIEW

END
VIEW

REIN
.020 ALUMINUM
(2 REQ'D)

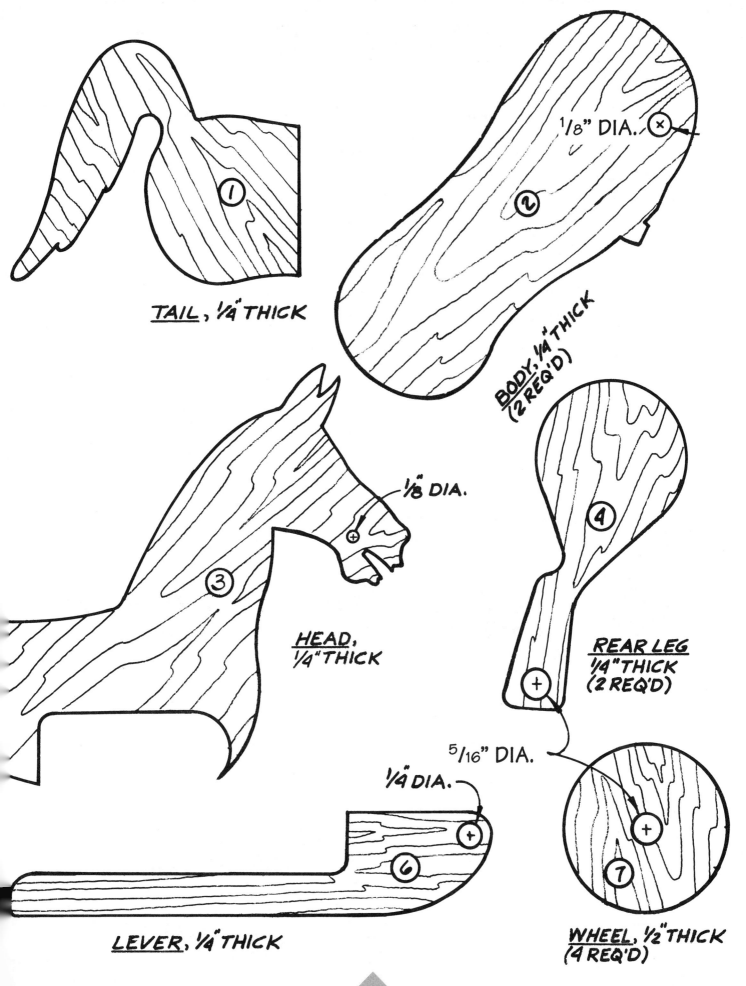

TAIL, 1/4" THICK

BODY, 1/4" THICK
(2 REQ'D)

1/8" DIA.

HEAD,
1/4" THICK

1/8" DIA.

REAR LEG
1/4" THICK
(2 REQ'D)

5/16" DIA.

1/4" DIA.

LEVER, 1/4" THICK

WHEEL, 1/2" THICK
(4 REQ'D)

DIVING FROG

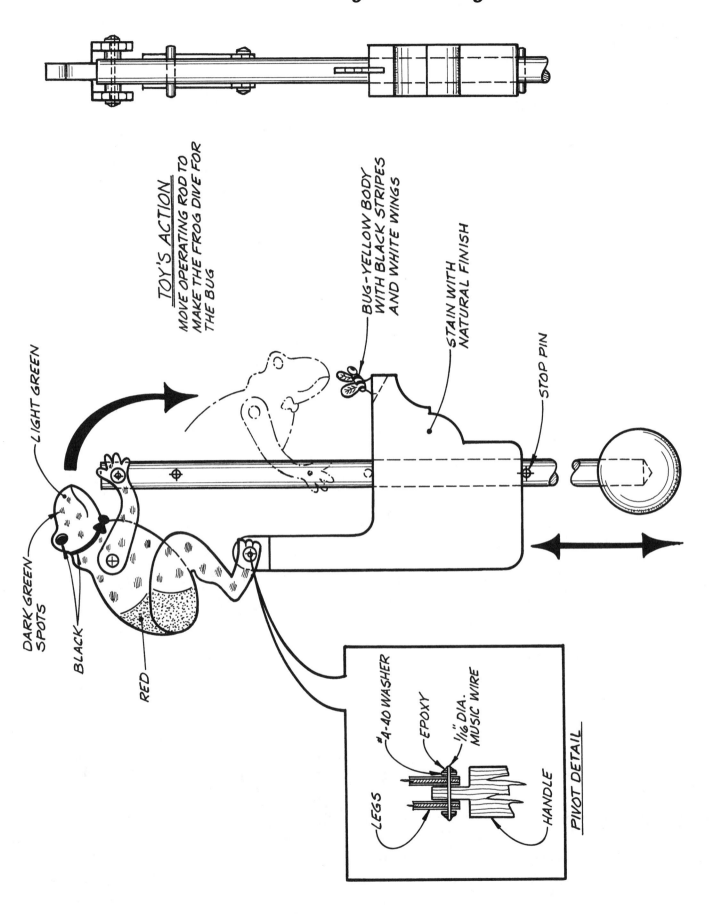

TOY'S ACTION
MOVE OPERATING ROD TO
MAKE THE FROG DIVE FOR
THE BUG

BUG-YELLOW BODY
WITH BLACK STRIPES
AND WHITE WINGS

STAIN WITH
NATURAL FINISH

STOP PIN

LIGHT GREEN

DARK GREEN
SPOTS

BLACK

RED

#4-40 WASHER

EPOXY

1/16" DIA.
MUSIC WIRE

LEGS

HANDLE

PIVOT DETAIL

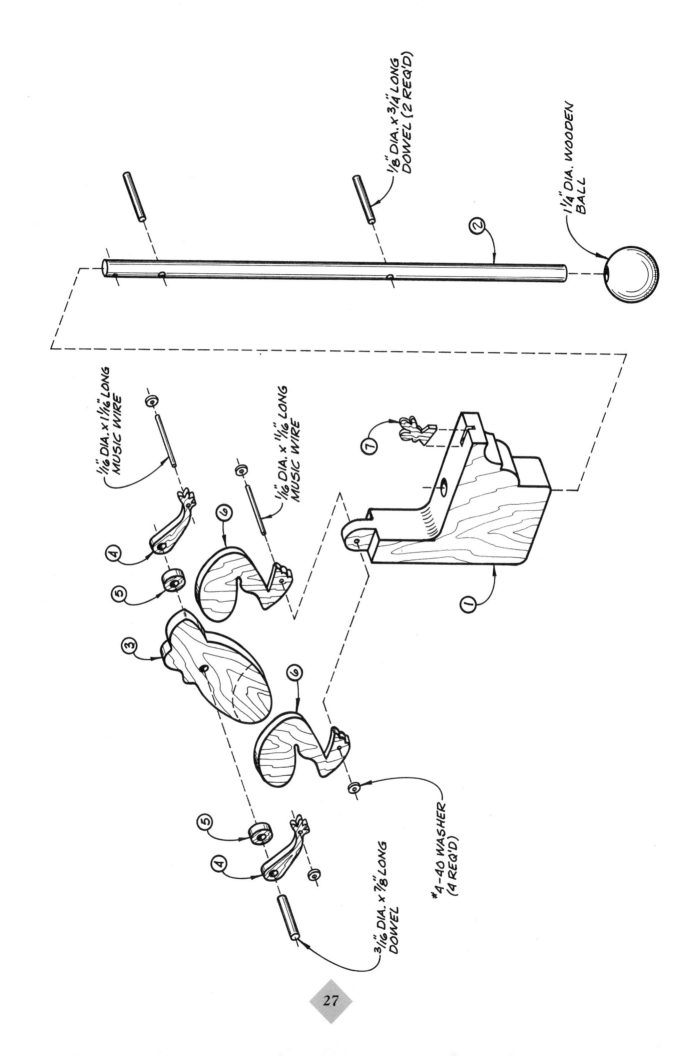

⅛" DIA. x ¾" LONG DOWEL (2 REQ'D)

1¼" DIA. WOODEN BALL

②

①

③

④

⑤

⑥

⑦

1/16" DIA. x 11/16" LONG MUSIC WIRE

1/16" DIA. x 11/16" LONG MUSIC WIRE

#4-40 WASHER (4 REQ'D)

3/16" DIA. x ⅞" LONG DOWEL

DIVING FROG
FULL-SIZE PATTERNS

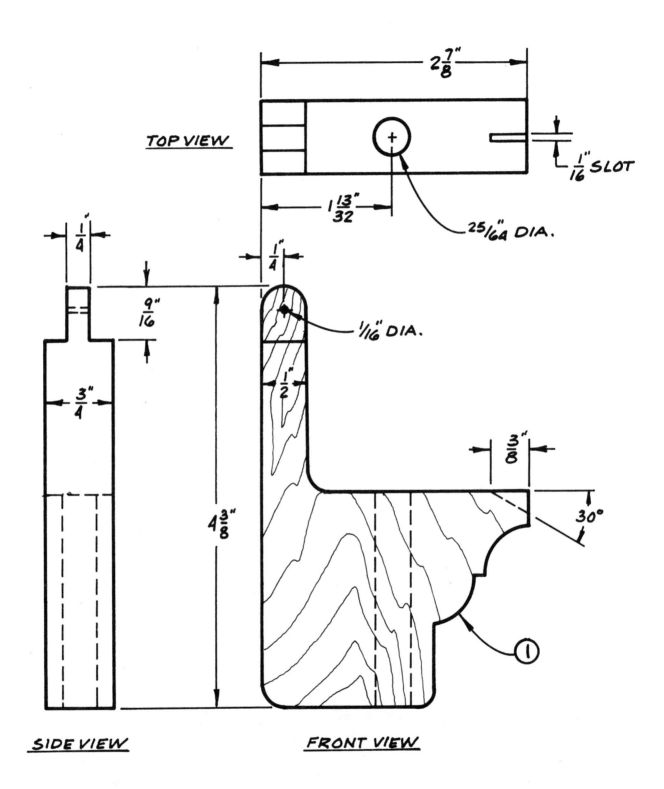

TOP VIEW

$2\frac{7}{8}"$

$\frac{1}{16}"$ SLOT

$1\frac{13}{32}"$

$25/64"$ DIA.

$\frac{1}{4}"$

$\frac{1}{4}"$

$\frac{9}{16}"$

$1/16"$ DIA.

$\frac{1}{2}"$

$\frac{3}{4}"$

$\frac{3}{8}"$

$30°$

$4\frac{3}{8}"$

①

SIDE VIEW

FRONT VIEW

HANDLE

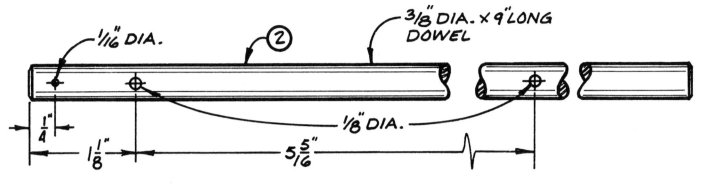

1/16" DIA.

② ③/8" DIA. × 9" LONG DOWEL

1/8" DIA.

1/4"

1 1/8"

5 5/16"

OPERATING ROD

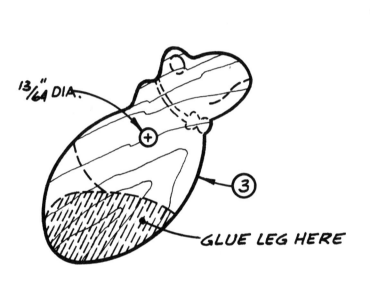

13/64 DIA.

③

GLUE LEG HERE

BODY
1/4" THICK

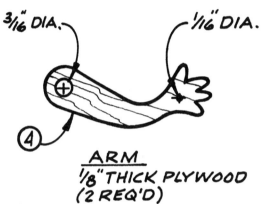

3/16" DIA.

1/16" DIA.

④

ARM
1/8" THICK PLYWOOD
(2 REQ'D)

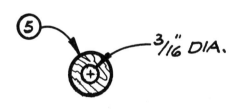

⑤ 3/16" DIA.

ARM SPACER
1/8" THICK PLYWOOD
(2 REQ'D)

⑦

BUG
1/16 THICK

⑥

LEG
1/8" THICK PLYWOOD
(2 REQ'D)

WALKING PIG

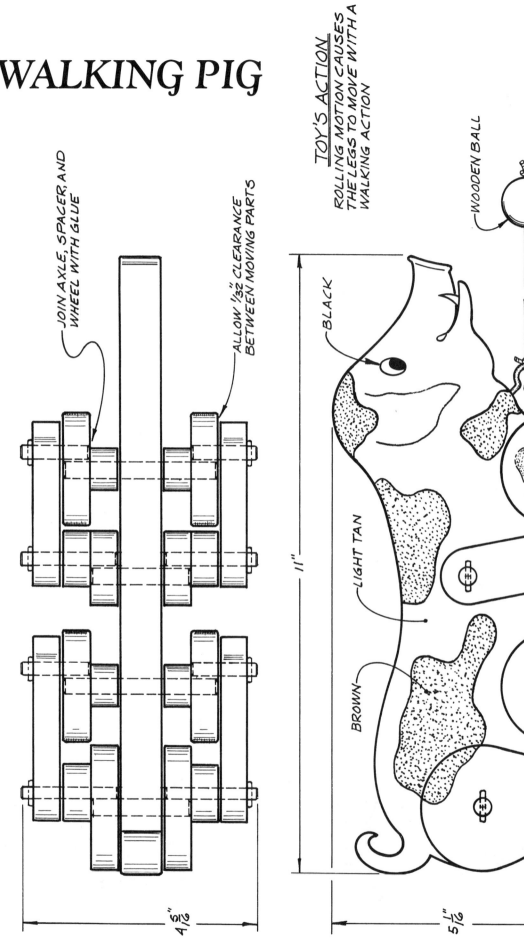

JOIN AXLE, SPACER, AND WHEEL WITH GLUE

ALLOW 1/32 CLEARANCE BETWEEN MOVING PARTS

4 5/16"

TOY'S ACTION

ROLLING MOTION CAUSES THE LEGS TO MOVE WITH A WALKING ACTION

WOODEN BALL

7/16" DIA. SCREW EYE

BLACK

LIGHT TAN

BROWN

BLACK

11"

5 1/2"

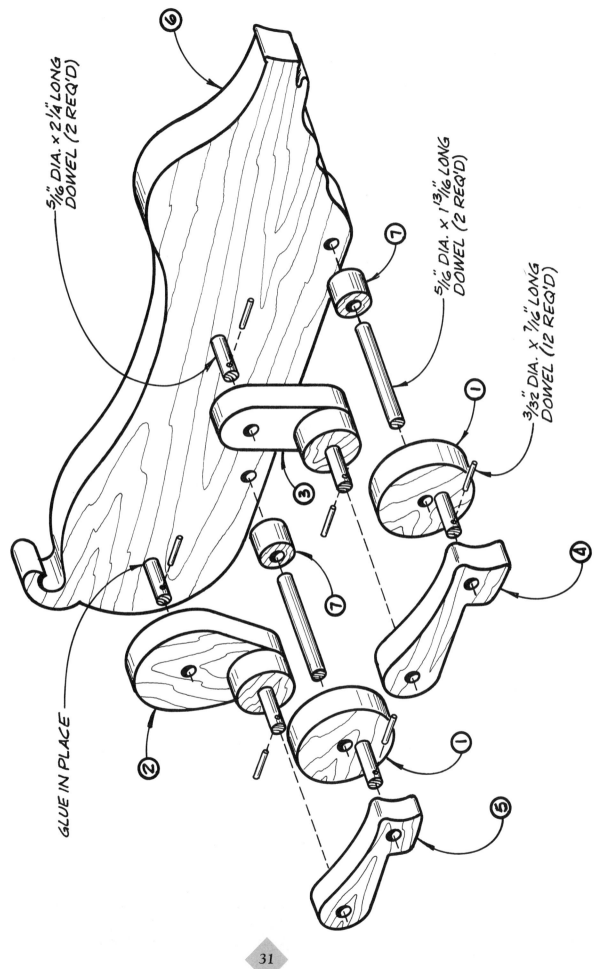

5/16" DIA. x 2 1/4" LONG DOWEL (2 REQ'D)

5/16" DIA. x 1 13/16" LONG DOWEL (2 REQ'D)

3/32 DIA. x 7/16" LONG DOWEL (12 REQ'D)

GLUE IN PLACE

31

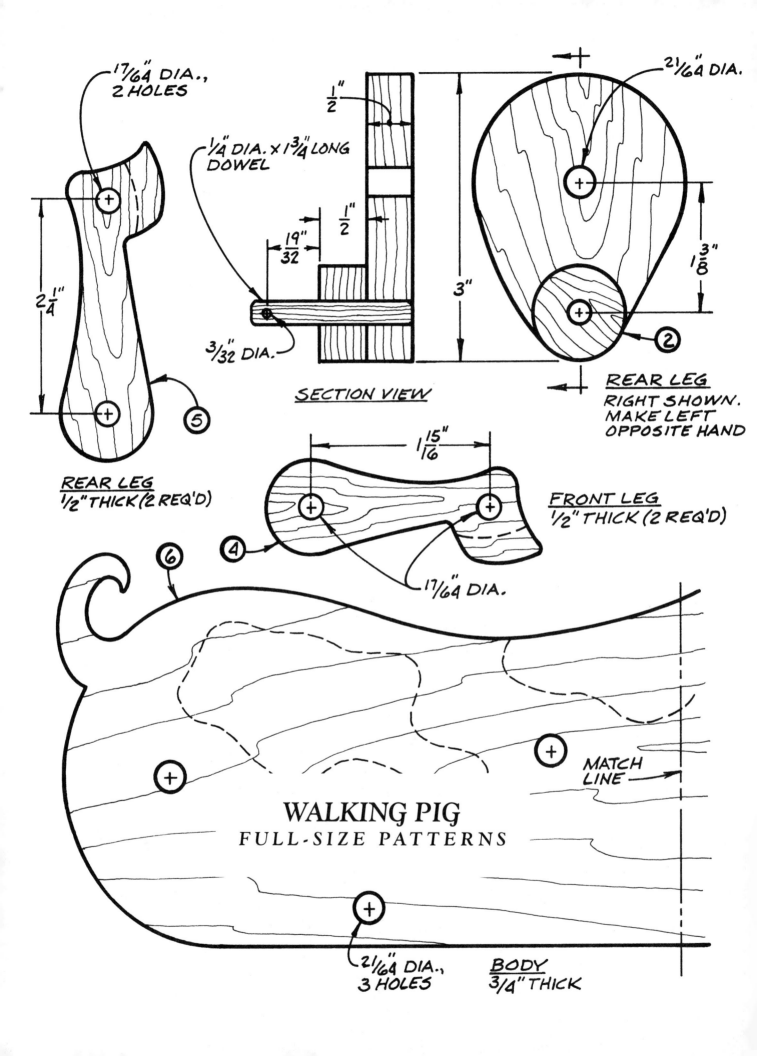

17/64" DIA., 2 HOLES

1/4" DIA. × 1 3/4" LONG DOWEL

3/32" DIA.

2 1/4"

REAR LEG
1/2" THICK (2 REQ'D)

5

SECTION VIEW

1/2"

1/2"

19/32"

3"

21/64 DIA.

1 3/8"

2

REAR LEG
RIGHT SHOWN.
MAKE LEFT
OPPOSITE HAND

1 15/16"

4

17/64" DIA.

FRONT LEG
1/2" THICK (2 REQ'D)

6

MATCH LINE

WALKING PIG
FULL-SIZE PATTERNS

21/64" DIA.,
3 HOLES

BODY
3/4" THICK

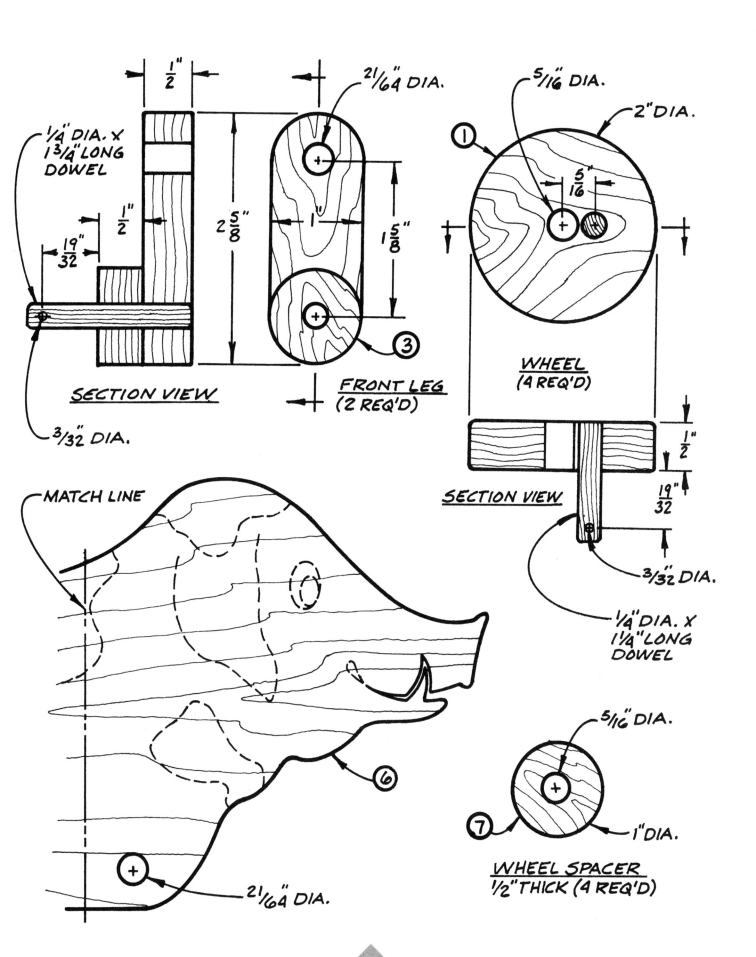

$\frac{1}{2}"$

$\frac{21}{64}$ DIA.

$\frac{5}{16}$ DIA.

2"DIA.

$\frac{1}{4}"$ DIA. X $1\frac{3}{4}"$LONG DOWEL

$\frac{1}{2}"$

①

$\frac{5}{16}$

$2\frac{5}{8}"$

$1"$

$1\frac{5}{8}"$

$\frac{19}{32}"$

③

$\frac{3}{32}"$ DIA.

SECTION VIEW

FRONT LEG
(2 REQ'D)

WHEEL
(4 REQ'D)

$\frac{1}{2}"$

$\frac{19}{32}"$

SECTION VIEW

$\frac{3}{32}"$ DIA.

$\frac{1}{4}"$DIA. X $1\frac{1}{4}"$LONG DOWEL

MATCH LINE

⑥

$\frac{5}{16}"$ DIA.

⑦

$1"$DIA.

+

$\frac{21}{64}"$ DIA.

WHEEL SPACER
$\frac{1}{2}"$THICK (4 REQ'D)

COURT JESTER

TOY'S ACTION

THE JESTER WILL SEEM TO
MAGICALLY CLING TO THE EDGE
OF A TABLE OR THE STAND AS
HE ROCKS BACK AND FORTH

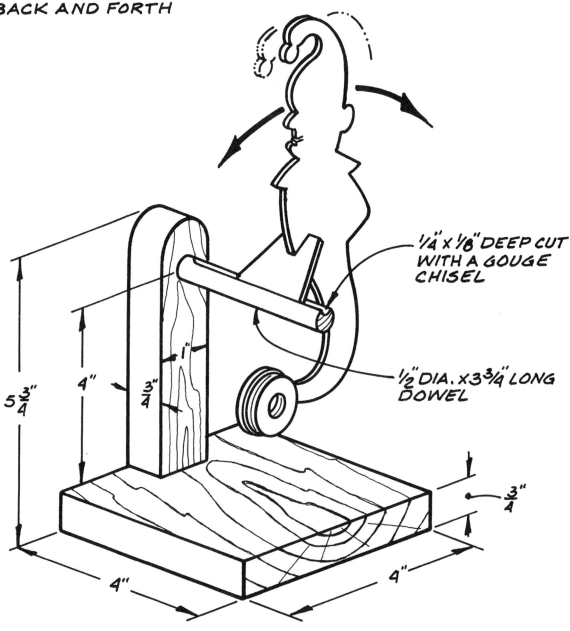

¼" X ⅛" DEEP CUT
WITH A GOUGE
CHISEL

½" DIA. X 3¾" LONG
DOWEL

5¾"

4"

3/4"

1"

4"

4"

3/4"

STAND

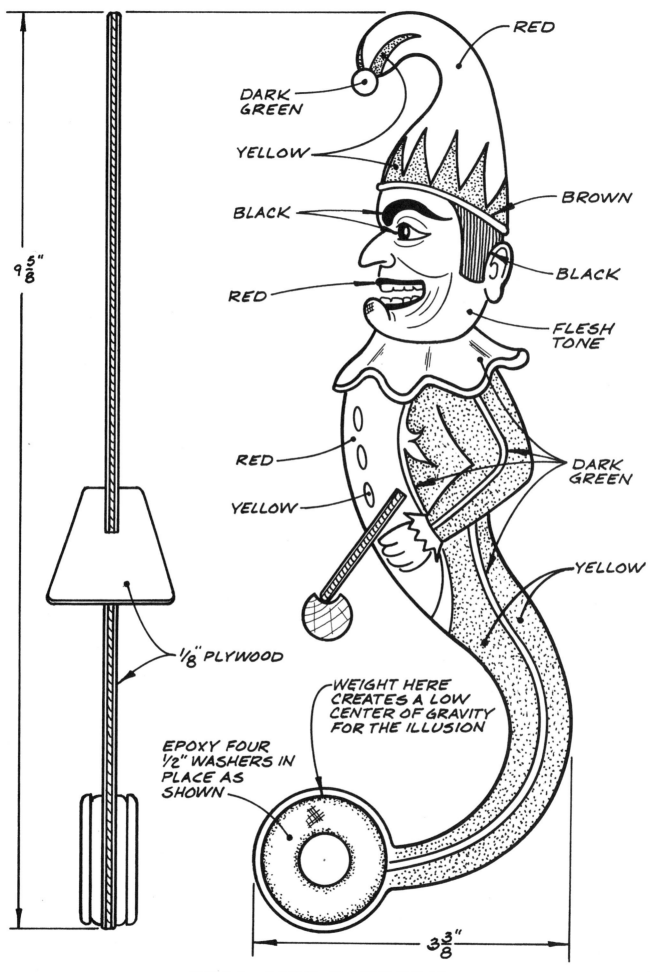

RED

DARK GREEN

YELLOW

BLACK

RED

BROWN

BLACK

FLESH TONE

RED

YELLOW

DARK GREEN

YELLOW

$9\frac{5}{8}"$

$\frac{1}{8}"$ PLYWOOD

WEIGHT HERE CREATES A LOW CENTER OF GRAVITY FOR THE ILLUSION

EPOXY FOUR $\frac{1}{2}"$ WASHERS IN PLACE AS SHOWN

$3\frac{3}{8}"$

FULL-SIZE PATTERN

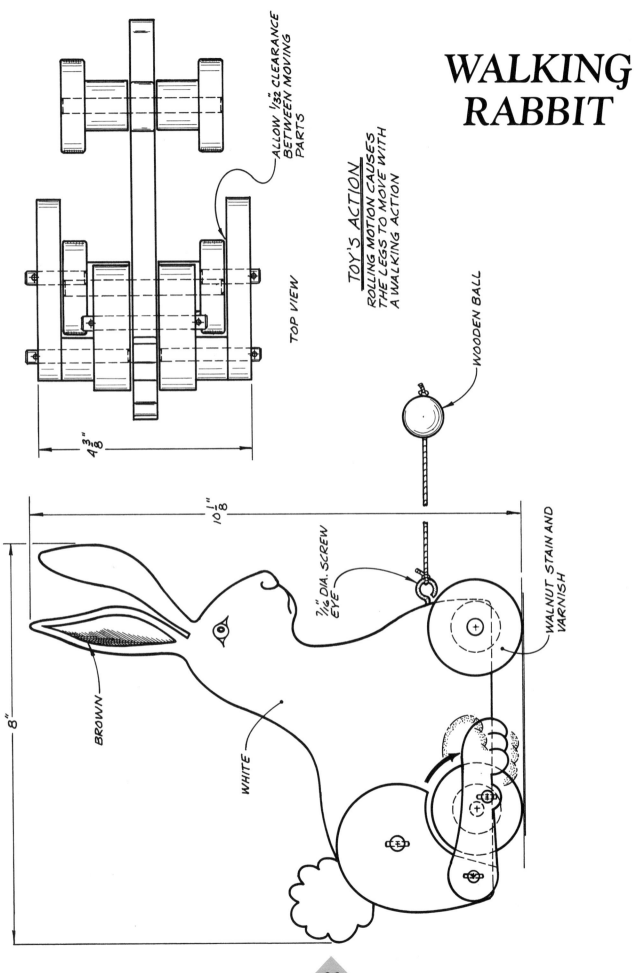

ALLOW 1/32" CLEARANCE BETWEEN MOVING PARTS

TOP VIEW

$4\frac{3}{8}$"

TOY'S ACTION
ROLLING MOTION CAUSES THE LEGS TO MOVE WITH A WALKING ACTION

WOODEN BALL

WALKING RABBIT

$10\frac{1}{8}$"

$\frac{7}{16}$" DIA. SCREW EYE

WALNUT STAIN AND VARNISH

BROWN

WHITE

8"

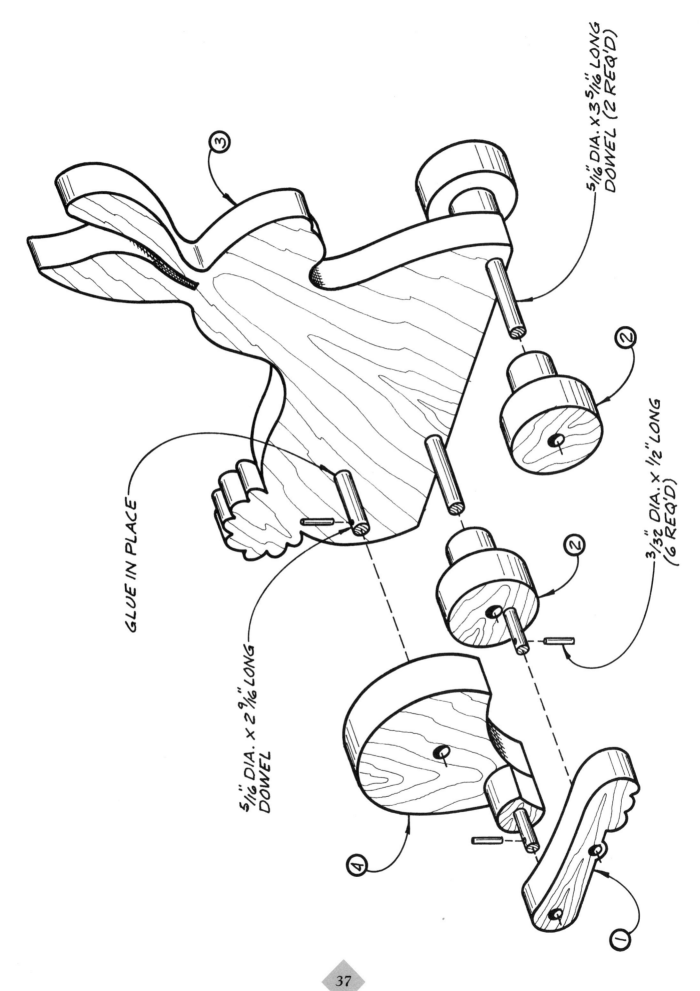

③

⑤⁄₁₆" DIA. × 3 ⁵⁄₁₆" LONG
DOWEL (2 REQ'D)

②

③⁄₃₂" DIA. × ½" LONG
(6 REQ'D)

②

GLUE IN PLACE

⑤⁄₁₆" DIA. × 2 ⁹⁄₁₆" LONG
DOWEL

④

①

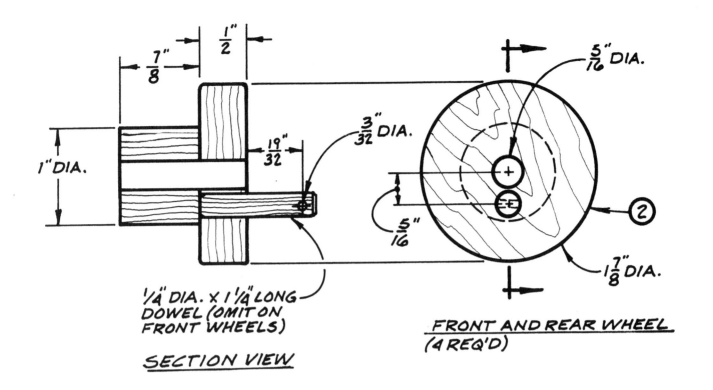

$\frac{7}{8}$" $\frac{1}{2}$"

1" DIA.

$\frac{19}{32}$"

$\frac{3}{32}$" DIA.

$\frac{5}{16}$" DIA.

$\frac{5}{16}$"

$1\frac{7}{8}$" DIA.

②

¼" DIA. X 1¼" LONG DOWEL (OMIT ON FRONT WHEELS)

SECTION VIEW

FRONT AND REAR WHEEL
(4 REQ'D)

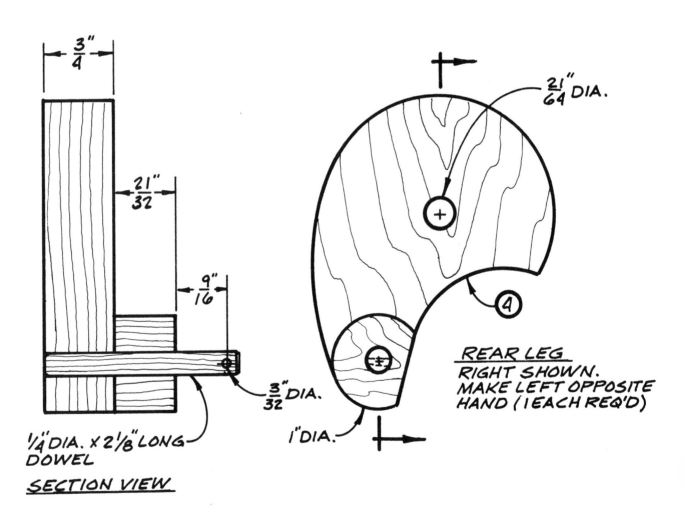

$\frac{3}{4}$"

$\frac{21}{32}$"

$\frac{9}{16}$"

$\frac{3}{32}$" DIA.

$\frac{21}{64}$" DIA.

④

1" DIA.

¼" DIA. X 2⅛" LONG DOWEL

SECTION VIEW

REAR LEG
RIGHT SHOWN.
MAKE LEFT OPPOSITE
HAND (1 EACH REQ'D)

WALKING RABBIT
FULL-SIZE PATTERNS

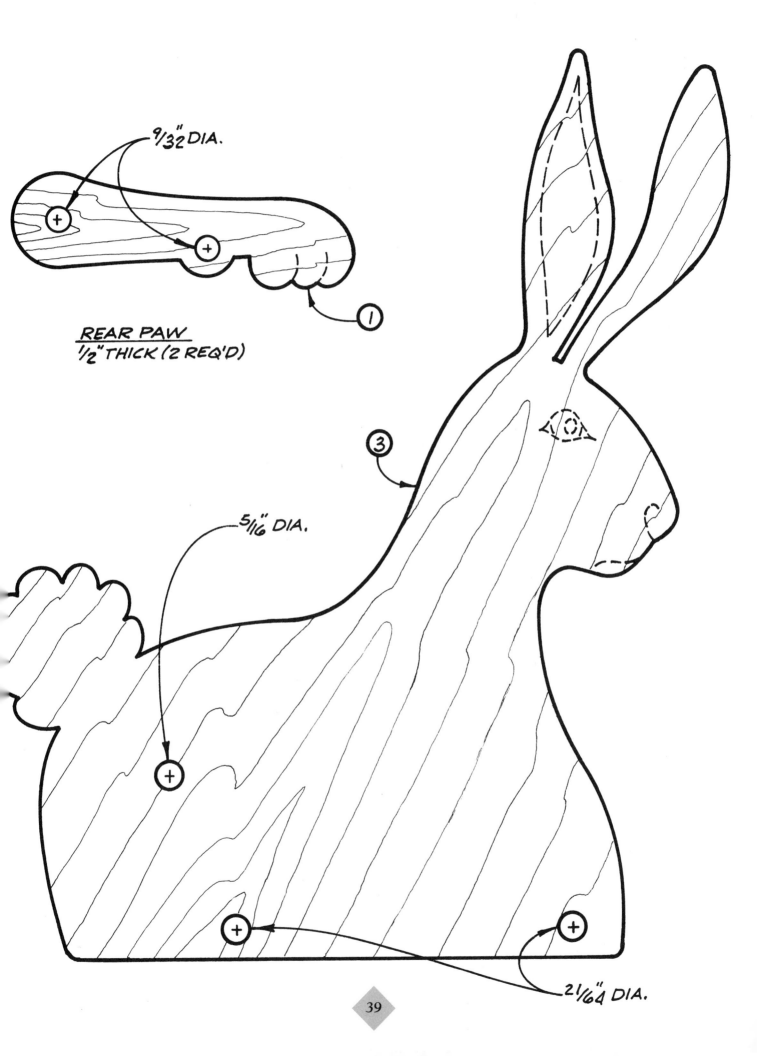

9/32" DIA.

REAR PAW
1/2" THICK (2 REQ'D)

1

5/16" DIA.

3

21/64" DIA.

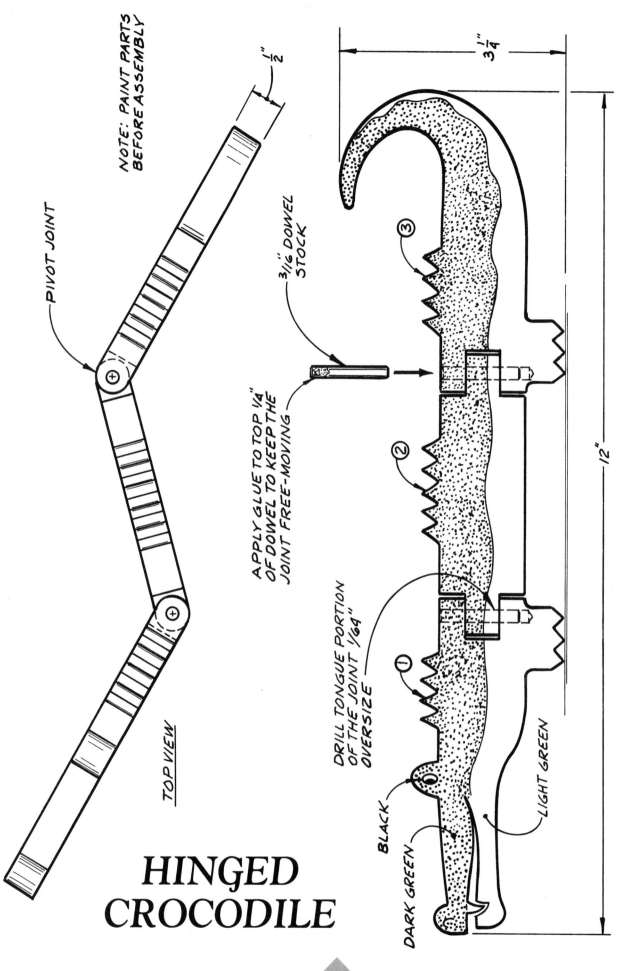

NOTE: PAINT PARTS BEFORE ASSEMBLY

PIVOT JOINT

TOP VIEW

$\frac{1}{2}$"

$3\frac{1}{4}$"

12"

$\frac{3}{16}$" DOWEL STOCK

APPLY GLUE TO TOP $\frac{1}{4}$" OF DOWEL TO KEEP THE JOINT FREE-MOVING

DRILL TONGUE PORTION OF THE JOINT $\frac{1}{64}$" OVERSIZE

③

②

①

BLACK

DARK GREEN

LIGHT GREEN

HINGED CROCODILE

FULL-SIZE PATTERNS

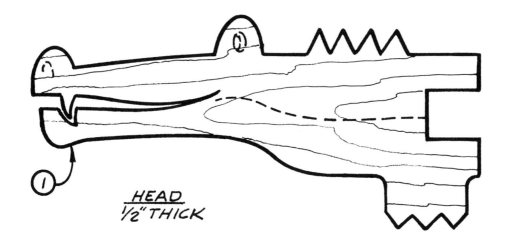

HEAD
1/2" THICK

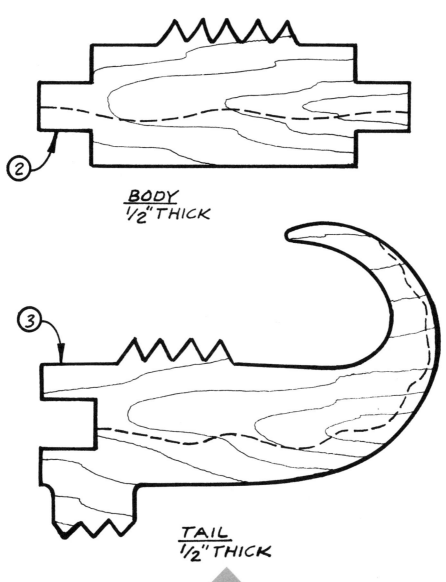

BODY
1/2" THICK

TAIL
1/2" THICK

LADY AND HER FLOCK

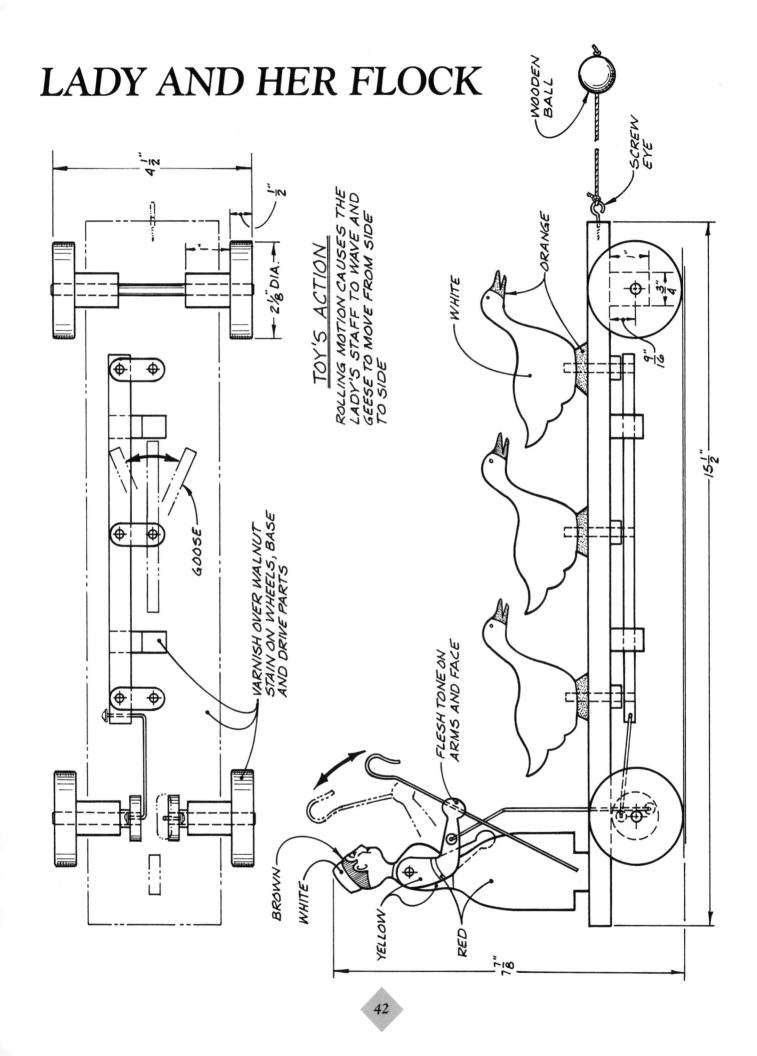

4 1/2"

1/2"

2 1/8" DIA.

GOOSE

VARNISH OVER WALNUT STAIN ON WHEELS, BASE AND DRIVE PARTS

WOODEN BALL

SCREW EYE

ORANGE

WHITE

TOY'S ACTION

ROLLING MOTION CAUSES THE LADY'S STAFF TO WAVE AND GEESE TO MOVE FROM SIDE TO SIDE

15 1/2"

3/4

9/16"

FLESH TONE ON ARMS AND FACE

BROWN

WHITE

YELLOW

RED

7 7/8"

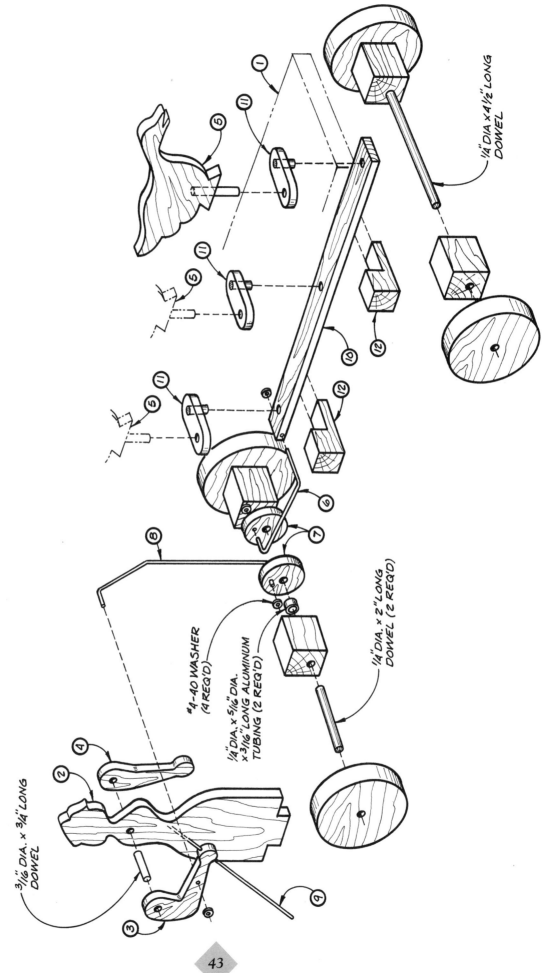

¼"DIA x4½" LONG DOWEL

#4-40 WASHER (4 REQ'D)

¼"DIA. x 5⁄16" DIA. x 3⁄16" LONG ALUMINUM TUBING (2 REQ'D)

¼" DIA. x 2" LONG DOWEL (2 REQ'D)

3⁄16" DIA. x ¾" LONG DOWEL

LADY AND HER FLOCK
FULL-SIZE PATTERNS

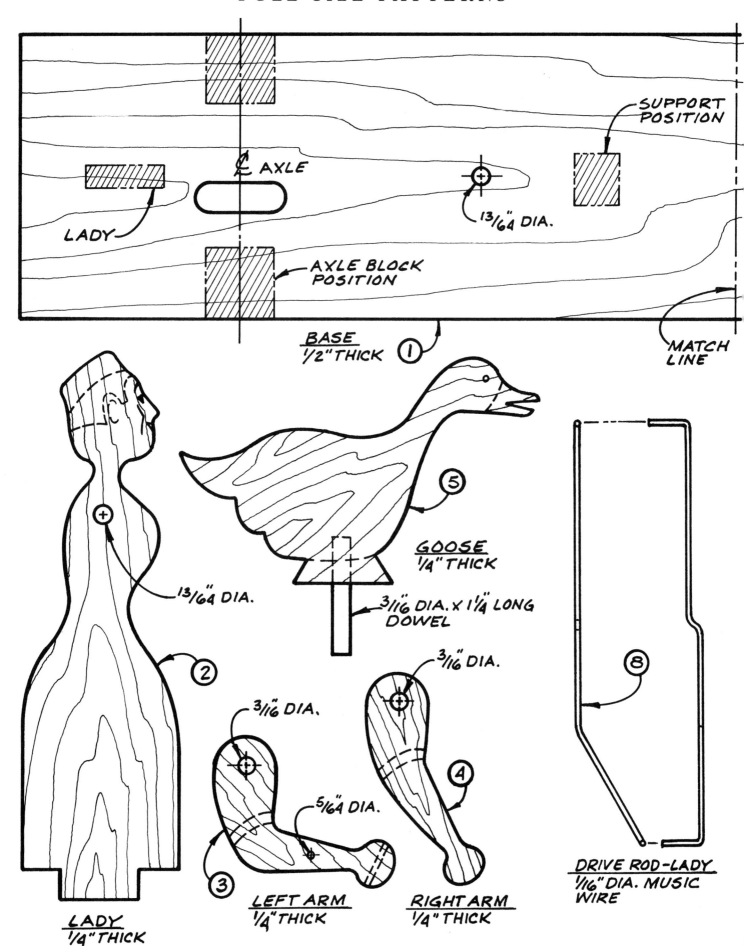

SUPPORT POSITION

₵ AXLE

LADY

13/64" DIA.

AXLE BLOCK POSITION

BASE 1/2" THICK ①

MATCH LINE

13/64" DIA.

②

LADY 1/4" THICK

GOOSE 1/4" THICK

⑤

3/16" DIA. x 1 1/4 LONG DOWEL

3/16" DIA.

3/16" DIA.

5/64" DIA.

③

④

LEFT ARM 1/4" THICK

RIGHT ARM 1/4" THICK

⑧

DRIVE ROD-LADY 1/16" DIA. MUSIC WIRE

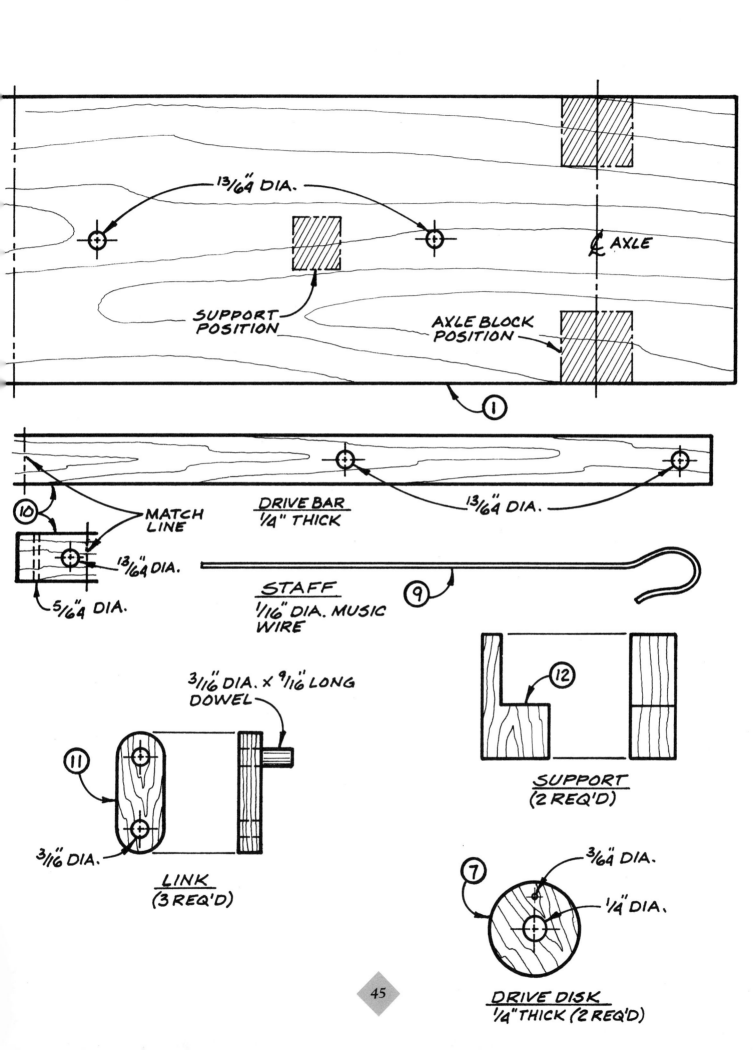

13/64" DIA.

♎ AXLE

SUPPORT
POSITION

AXLE BLOCK
POSITION

①

DRIVE BAR
1/4" THICK

13/64" DIA.

⑩

MATCH
LINE

13/64" DIA.

5/64" DIA.

STAFF
1/16" DIA. MUSIC
WIRE

⑨

3/16" DIA. × 9/16" LONG
DOWEL

⑫

⑪

3/16" DIA.

LINK
(3 REQ'D)

SUPPORT
(2 REQ'D)

3/64" DIA.

1/4" DIA.

⑦

DRIVE DISK
1/4" THICK (2 REQ'D)

45

HINGED SNAKE

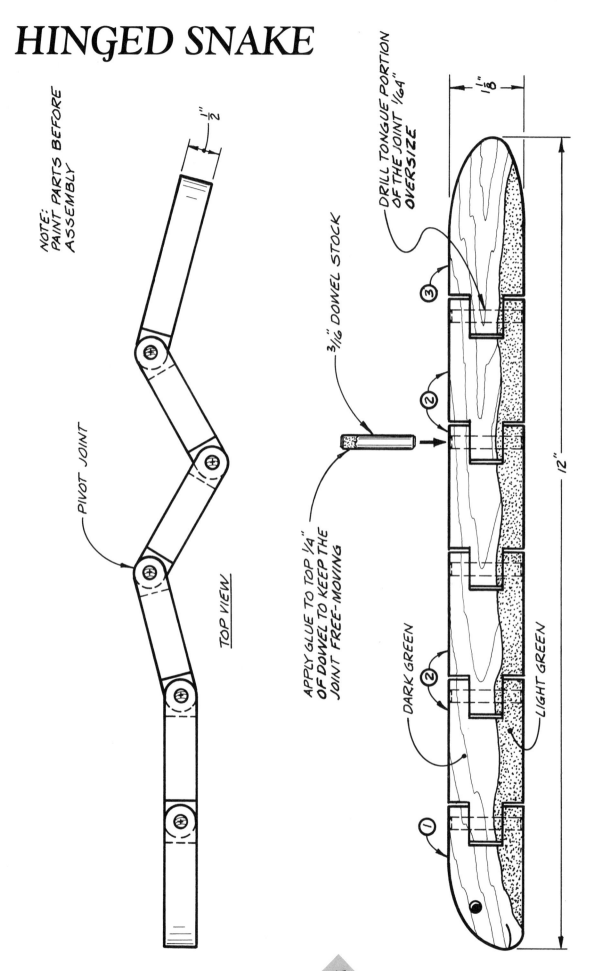

NOTE:
PAINT PARTS BEFORE
ASSEMBLY

PIVOT JOINT

TOP VIEW

$\frac{1}{2}$"

3/16" DOWEL STOCK

APPLY GLUE TO TOP 1/4"
OF DOWEL TO KEEP THE
JOINT FREE-MOVING

DRILL TONGUE PORTION
OF THE JOINT 1/64"
OVERSIZE

1$\frac{1}{8}$"

12"

DARK GREEN

LIGHT GREEN

1

2

3

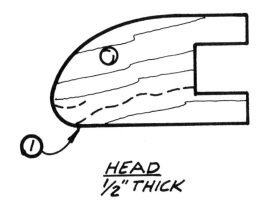

HEAD
½" THICK

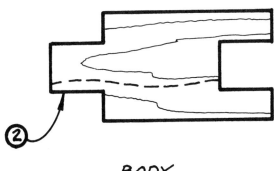

BODY
½" THICK (4 REQ'D)

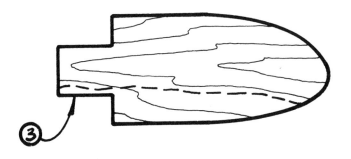

TAIL
½" THICK

FLYING CHICKEN

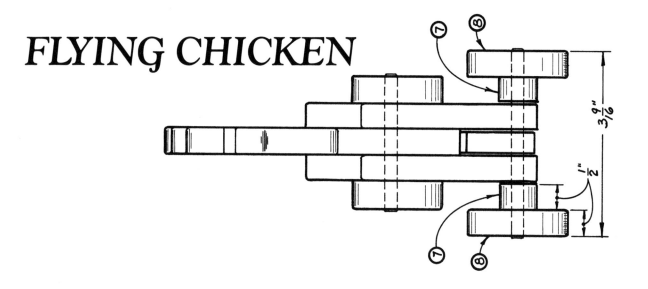

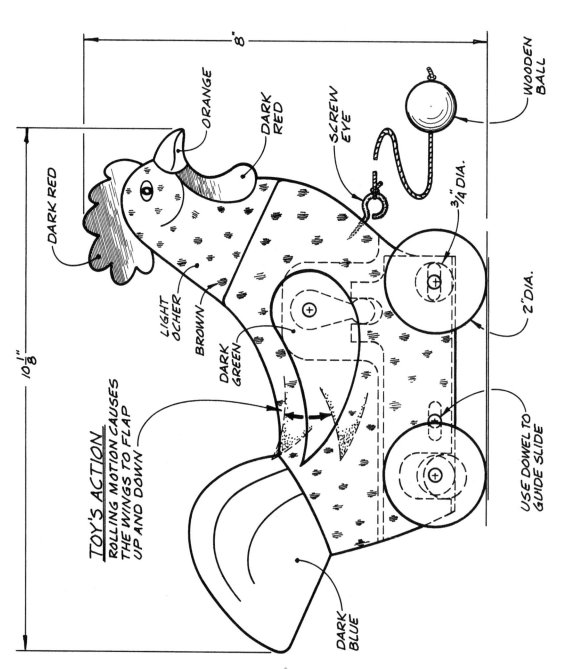

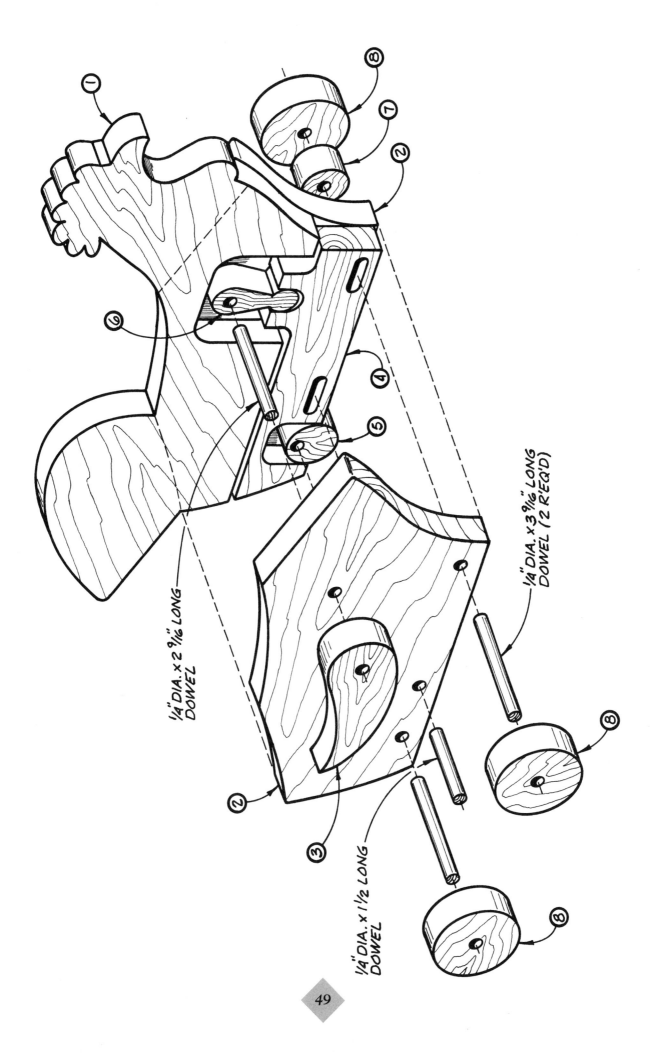

¼" DIA. x 2 9/16" LONG
DOWEL

¼" DIA. x 3 9/16" LONG
DOWEL (2 R'EQD)

¼" DIA. x 1½" LONG
DOWEL

49

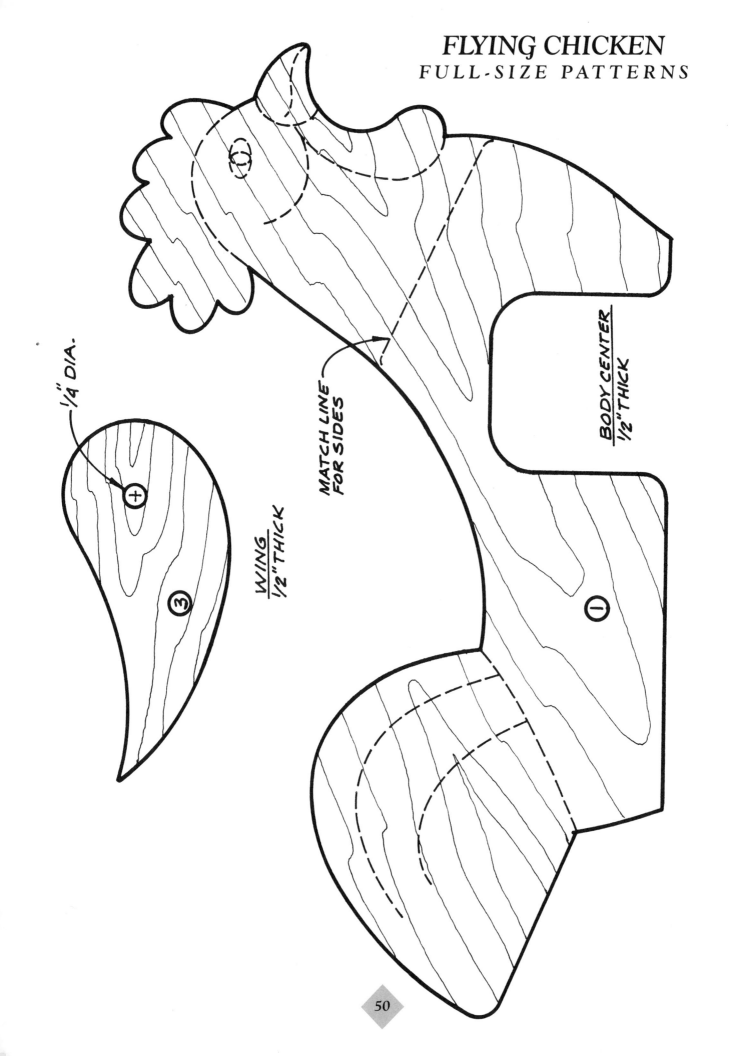

FLYING CHICKEN
FULL-SIZE PATTERNS

WING
½" THICK

MATCH LINE FOR SIDES

BODY CENTER
½" THICK

¼" DIA.

50

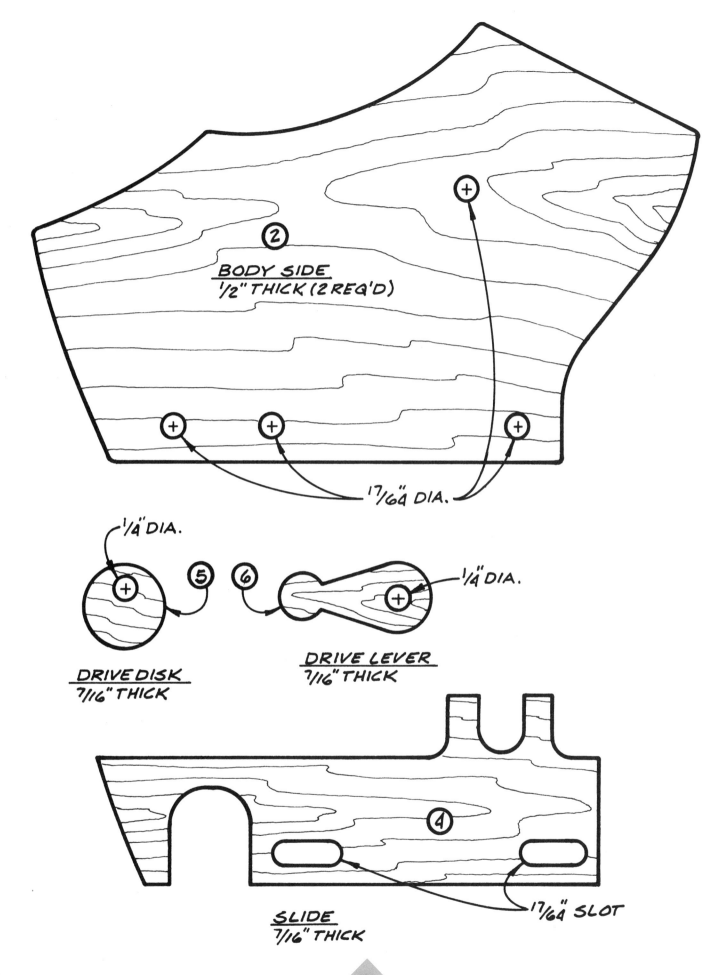

② BODY SIDE
1/2" THICK (2 REQ'D)

17/64" DIA.

1/4" DIA.

⑤ DRIVE DISK
7/16" THICK

⑥ DRIVE LEVER
7/16" THICK

1/4" DIA.

④ SLIDE
7/16" THICK

17/64" SLOT

CLIMBING MONKEY

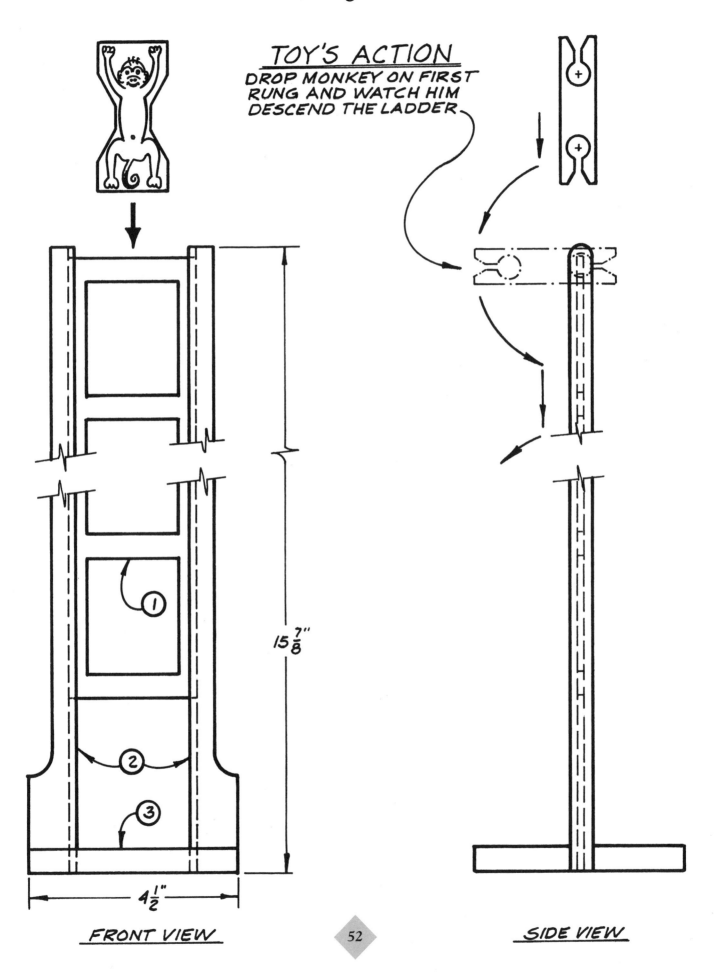

TOY'S ACTION
DROP MONKEY ON FIRST
RUNG AND WATCH HIM
DESCEND THE LADDER

$15\frac{7}{8}''$

$4\frac{1}{2}''$

FRONT VIEW

SIDE VIEW

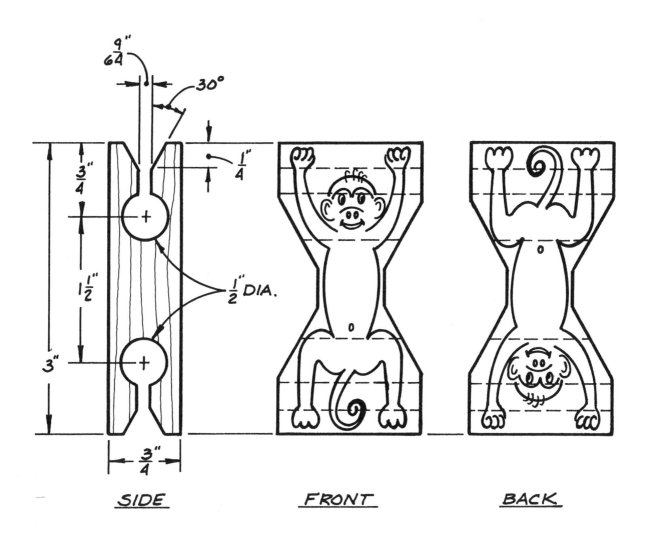

SIDE   FRONT   BACK

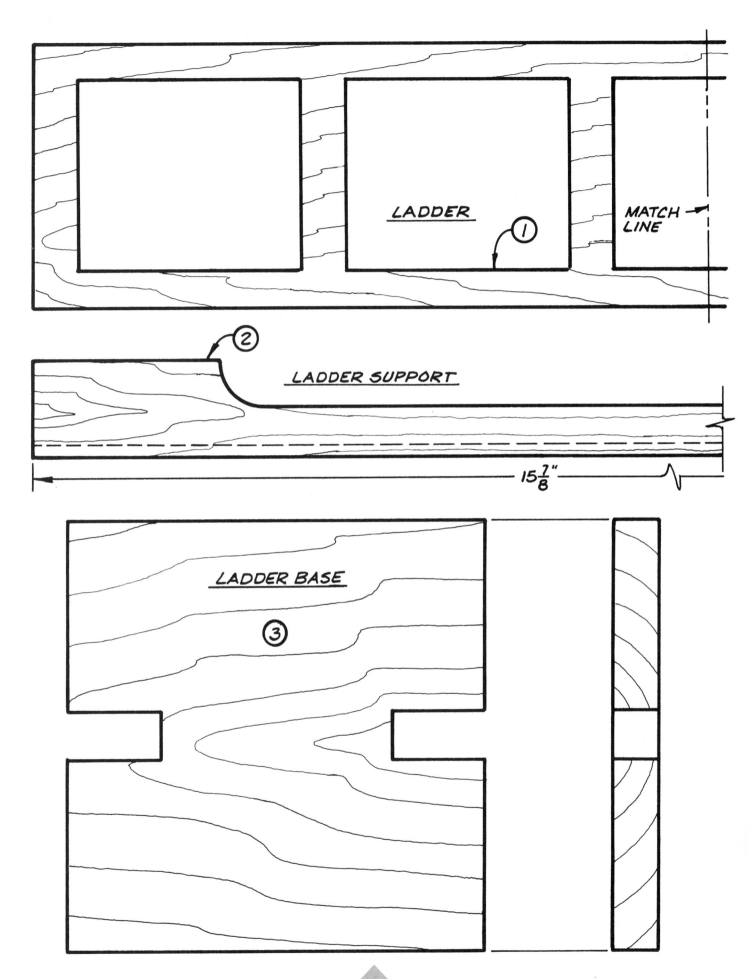

LADDER ①

MATCH LINE →

② LADDER SUPPORT

$15\frac{7}{8}"$

LADDER BASE ③

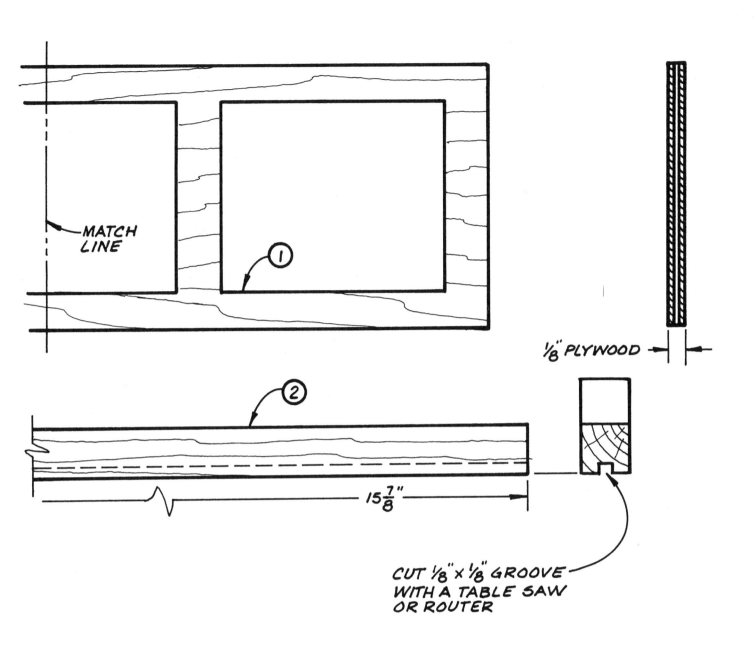

MATCH LINE

①

② 15 7/8"

1/8" PLYWOOD

CUT 1/8" x 1/8" GROOVE
WITH A TABLE SAW
OR ROUTER

CLIMBING MONKEY
FULL-SIZE PATTERNS

PEDALING CYCLIST

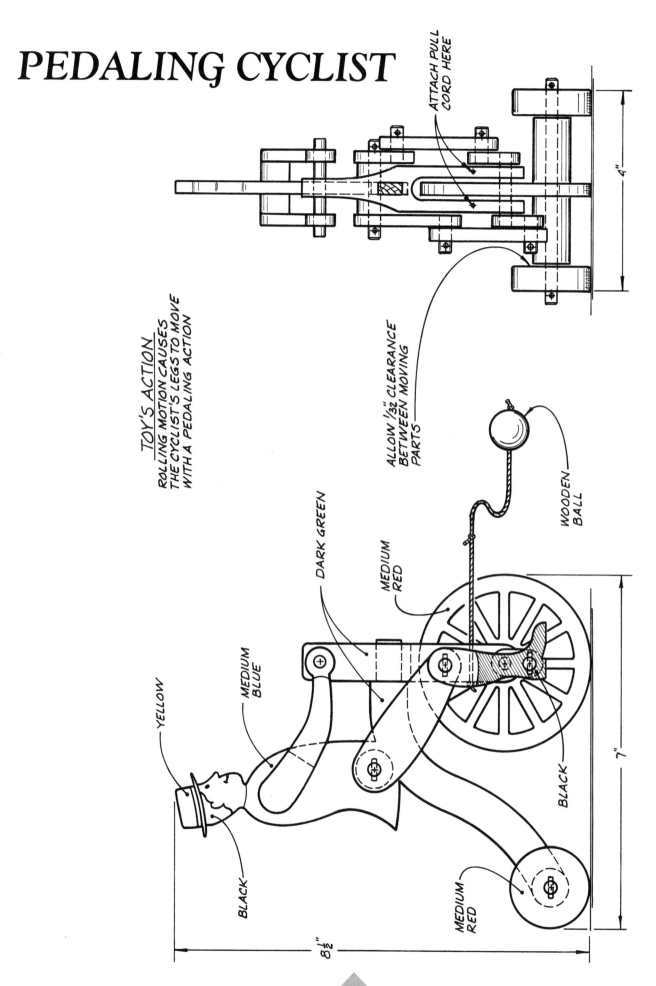

ATTACH PULL CORD HERE

4"

TOY'S ACTION
ROLLING MOTION CAUSES
THE CYCLIST'S LEGS TO MOVE
WITH A PEDALING ACTION

ALLOW 1/32" CLEARANCE BETWEEN MOVING PARTS

WOODEN BALL

DARK GREEN

MEDIUM RED

MEDIUM BLUE

YELLOW

BLACK

BLACK

7"

MEDIUM RED

8 1/2"

56

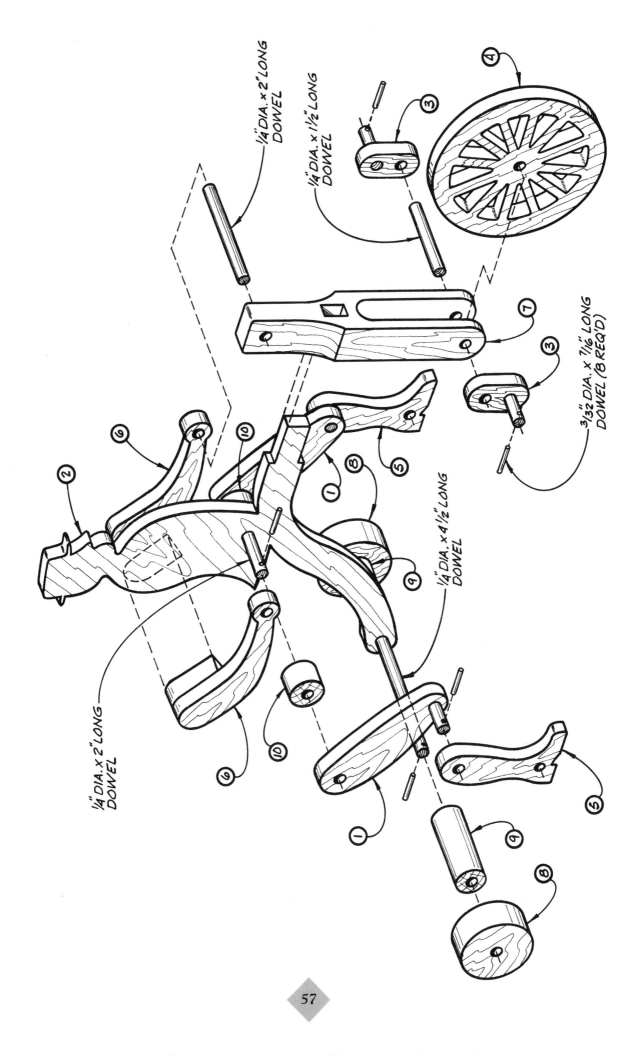

¼" DIA. x 2" LONG
DOWEL

¼" DIA. x 1½ LONG
DOWEL

3/32" DIA. x 7/16" LONG
DOWEL (8 REQ'D)

¼" DIA. x 4½" LONG
DOWEL

¼" DIA. x 2" LONG
DOWEL

57

PEDALING CYCLIST
FULL-SIZE PATTERNS

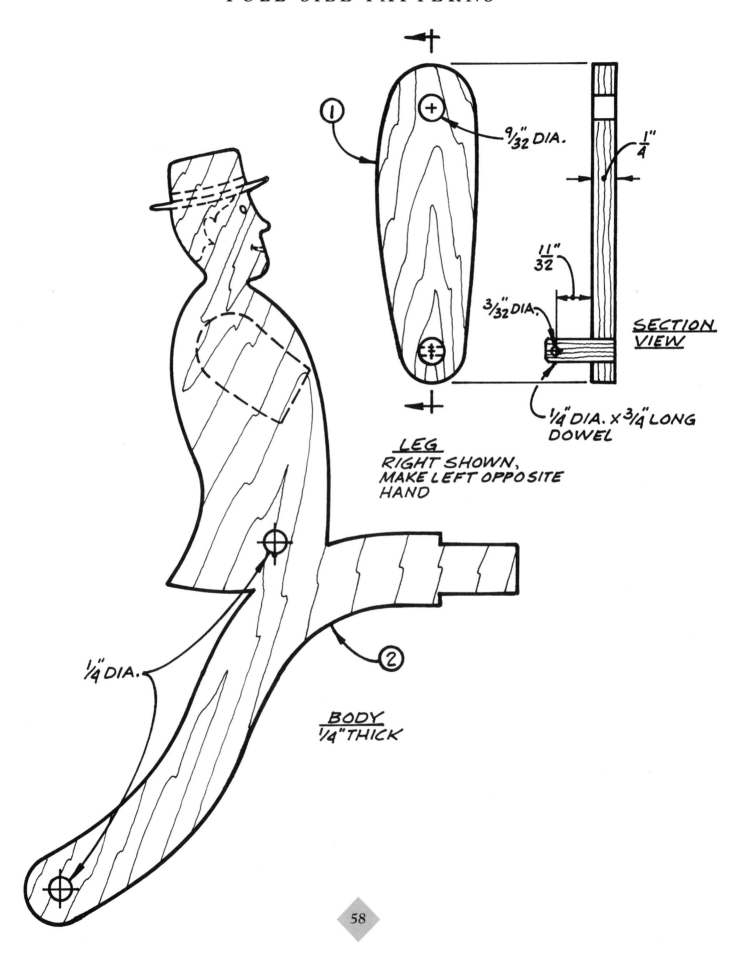

① $\frac{9}{32}$" DIA.

$\frac{1}{4}$"

SECTION VIEW

$\frac{11}{32}$"

$\frac{3}{32}$" DIA.

$\frac{1}{4}$" DIA. X $\frac{3}{4}$" LONG DOWEL

LEG
RIGHT SHOWN,
MAKE LEFT OPPOSITE
HAND

$\frac{1}{4}$" DIA.

②

BODY
$\frac{1}{4}$" THICK

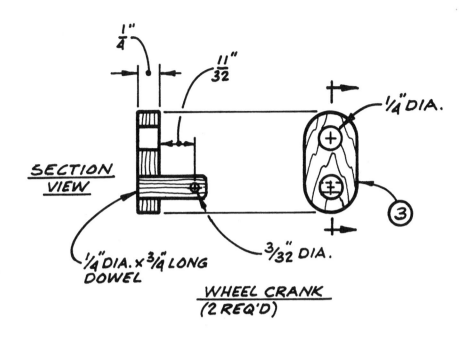

$\frac{1}{4}"$

$\frac{11}{32}"$

$\frac{1}{4}"$ DIA.

SECTION VIEW

$\frac{1}{4}"$ DIA. × $\frac{3}{4}"$ LONG DOWEL

$\frac{3}{32}"$ DIA.

③

WHEEL CRANK
(2 REQ'D)

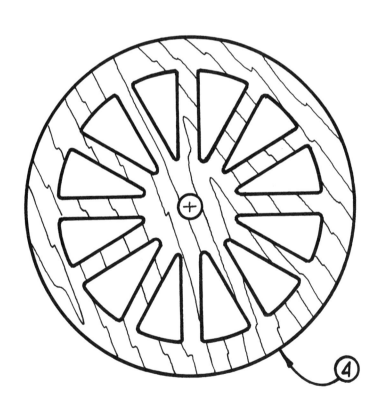

④

FRONT WHEEL
$\frac{1}{4}"$ THICK

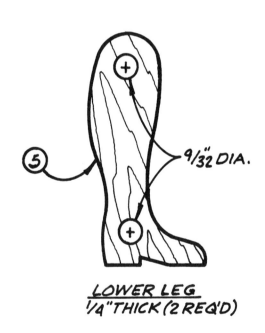

⑤

$\frac{9}{32}"$ DIA.

LOWER LEG
$\frac{1}{4}"$ THICK (2 REQ'D)

PEDALING CYCLIST
FULL-SIZE PATTERNS

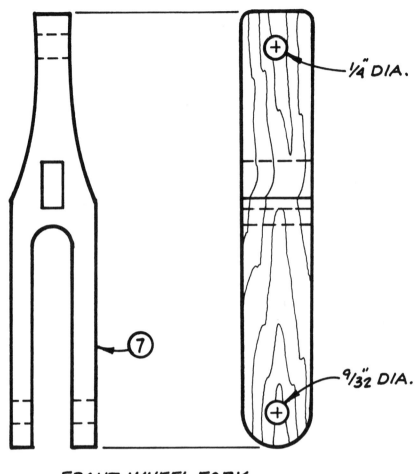

¼" DIA.

9/32" DIA.

⑦

FRONT WHEEL FORK

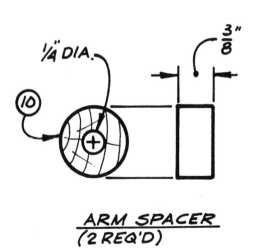

¼" DIA.

3/8"

⑩

ARM SPACER
(2 REQ'D)

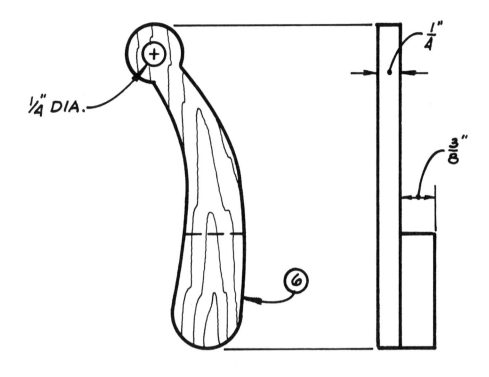

$\frac{1}{4}''$

$\frac{3}{8}''$

$\frac{1}{4}''$ DIA.

6

ARM
RIGHT SHOWN,
MAKE LEFT OPPOSITE
HAND

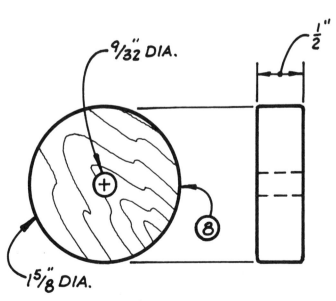

$\frac{1}{2}''$

$\frac{9}{32}''$ DIA.

8

$1\frac{5}{8}''$ DIA.

REAR WHEEL
(2 REQ'D)

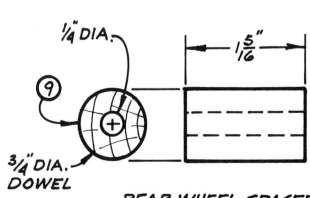

$\frac{1}{4}''$ DIA.

$1\frac{5}{16}''$

9

$\frac{3}{4}''$ DIA.
DOWEL

REAR WHEEL SPACER
(2 REQ'D)

WALKING
CROCODILE

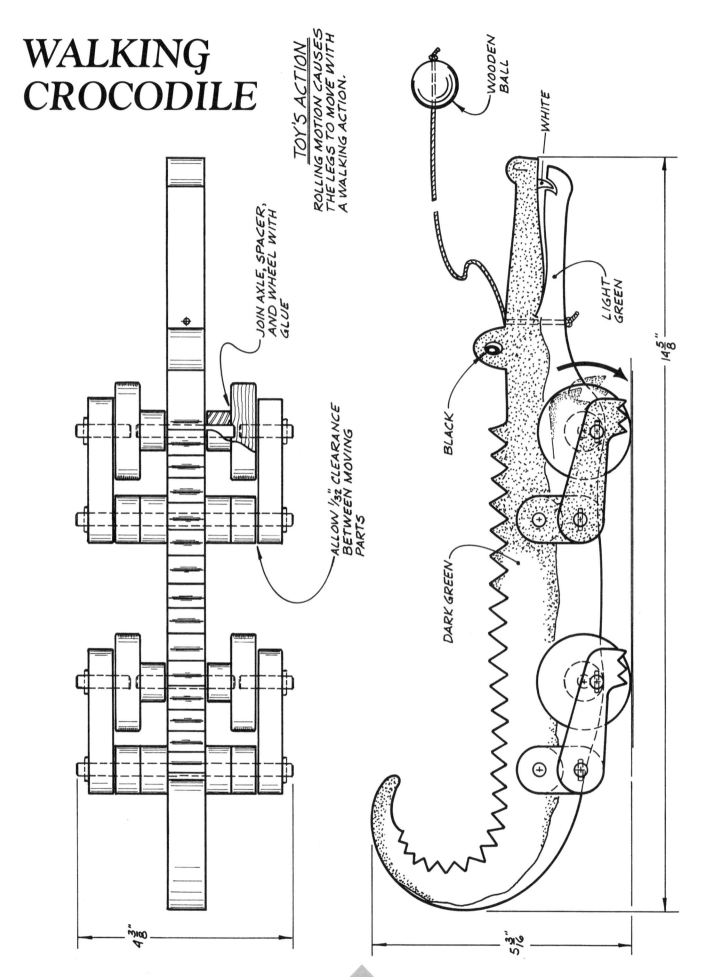

TOY'S ACTION

ROLLING MOTION CAUSES
THE LEGS TO MOVE WITH
A WALKING ACTION.

WOODEN
BALL

WHITE

JOIN AXLE, SPACER,
AND WHEEL WITH
GLUE

LIGHT
GREEN

ALLOW 1/32" CLEARANCE
BETWEEN MOVING
PARTS

BLACK

DARK GREEN

14 5/8"

5 3/16"

4 3/8"

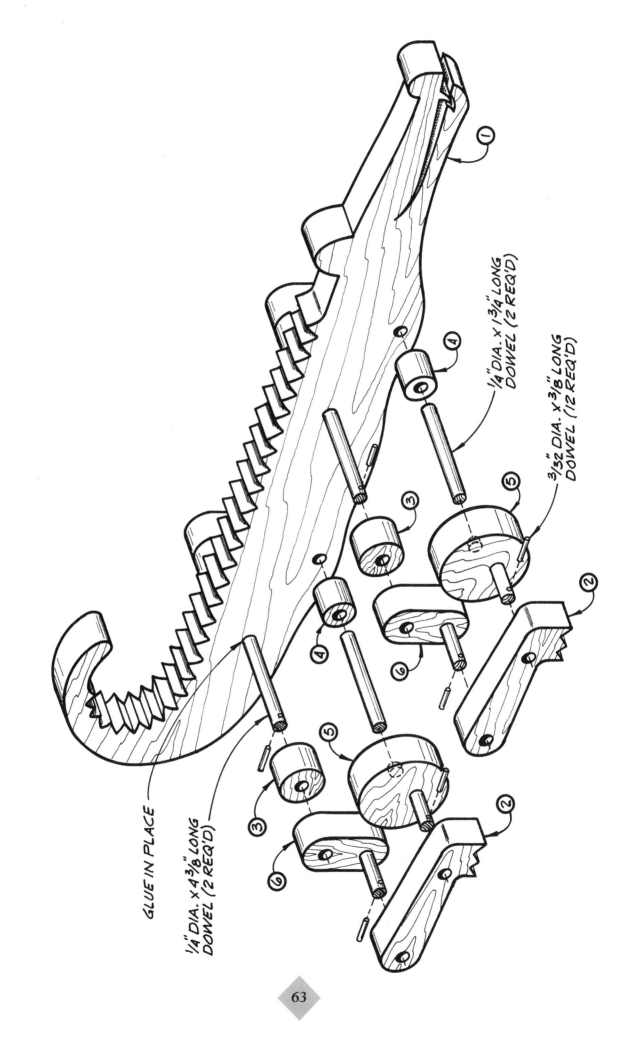

¼" DIA. x 1¾" LONG
DOWEL (2 REQ'D)

³⁄₃₂" DIA. x ³⁄₈" LONG
DOWEL (12 REQ'D)

GLUE IN PLACE

¼" DIA. x 4³⁄₈" LONG
DOWEL (2 REQ'D)

WALKING CROCODILE
FULL-SIZE PATTERNS

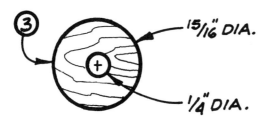

③ — 15/16" DIA. — 1/4" DIA.

ARM SPACER
1/2" THICK (4 REQ'D)

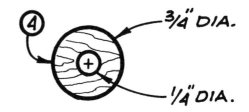

④ — 3/4" DIA. — 1/4" DIA.

WHEEL SPACER
1/2" THICK (4 REQ'D)

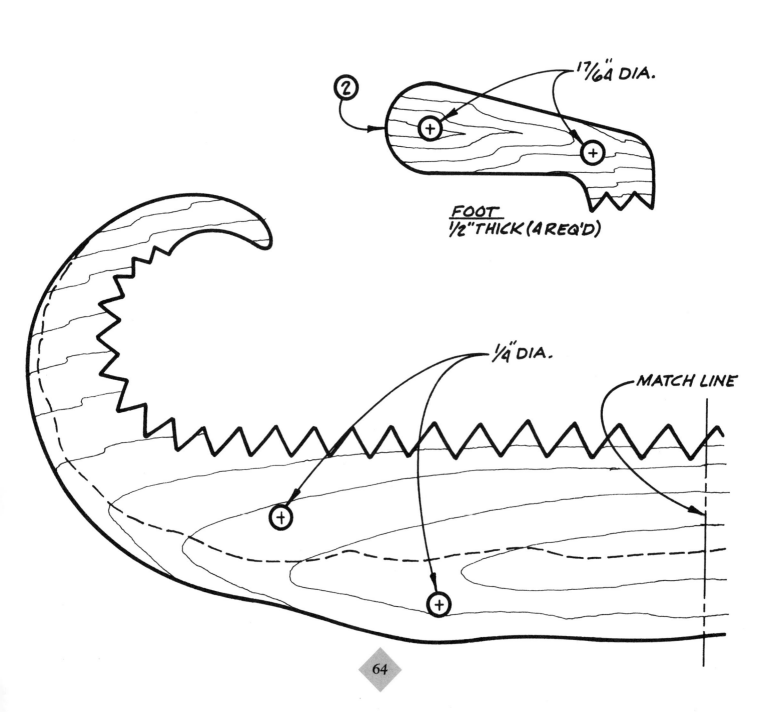

② — 17/64" DIA.

FOOT
1/2" THICK (4 REQ'D)

1/4" DIA.

MATCH LINE

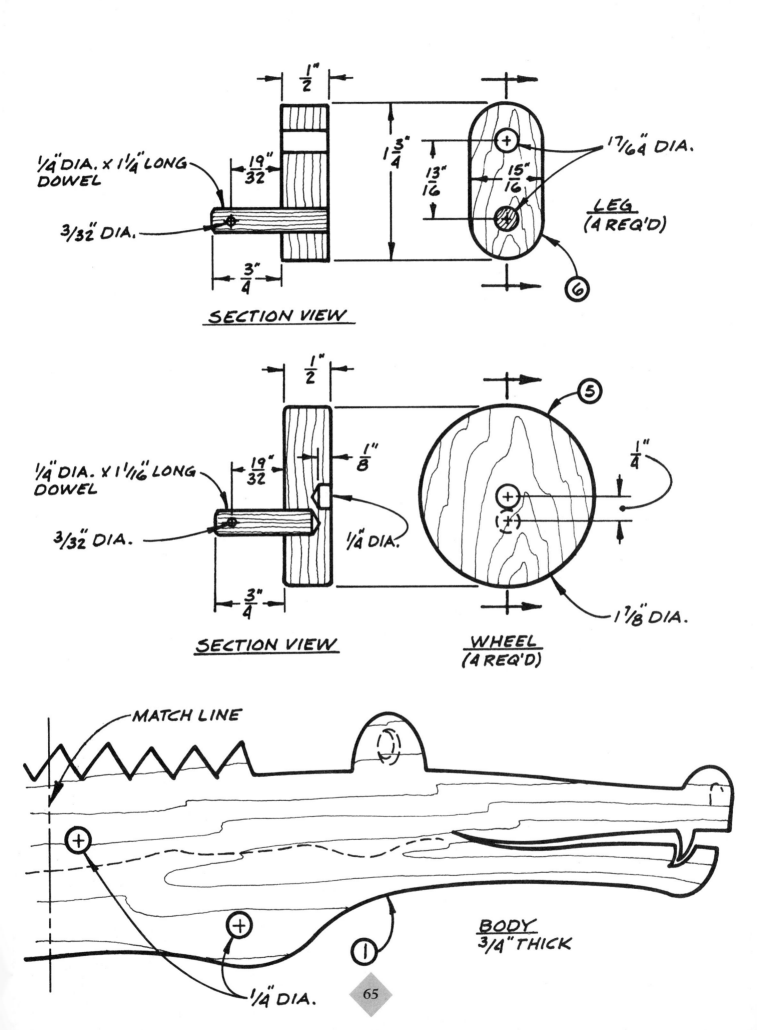

1/4" DIA. X 1 1/4" LONG DOWEL

3/32" DIA.

1/2"

19/32"

3/4"

1 3/4"

13/16"

15/16"

17/64" DIA.

LEG
(4 REQ'D)

⑥

SECTION VIEW

1/4" DIA. X 1 1/16" LONG DOWEL

3/32" DIA.

1/2"

19/32"

3/4"

1/8"

1/4" DIA.

⑤

1/4"

1 7/8" DIA.

WHEEL
(4 REQ'D)

SECTION VIEW

MATCH LINE

BODY
3/4" THICK

1/4" DIA.

①

65

HAND-POWERED RAILCAR

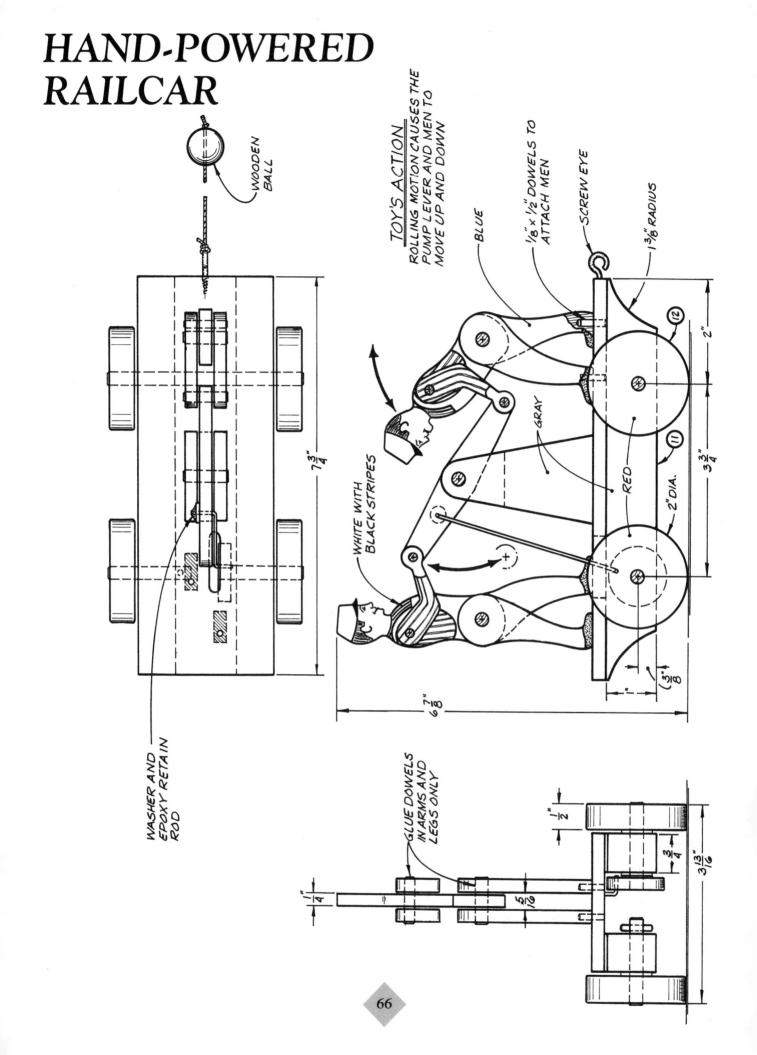

WOODEN BALL

WASHER AND EPOXY RETAIN ROD

TOY'S ACTION
ROLLING MOTION CAUSES THE PUMP LEVER AND MEN TO MOVE UP AND DOWN

BLUE

⅛" × ½" DOWELS TO ATTACH MEN

SCREW EYE

1⅜" RADIUS

GRAY

RED

2" DIA.

WHITE WITH BLACK STRIPES

12

11

7¾"

3¾"

2"

6⅞"

(⅜")

GLUE DOWELS IN ARMS AND LEGS ONLY

¼"

5/16"

½"

¾"

3 13/16"

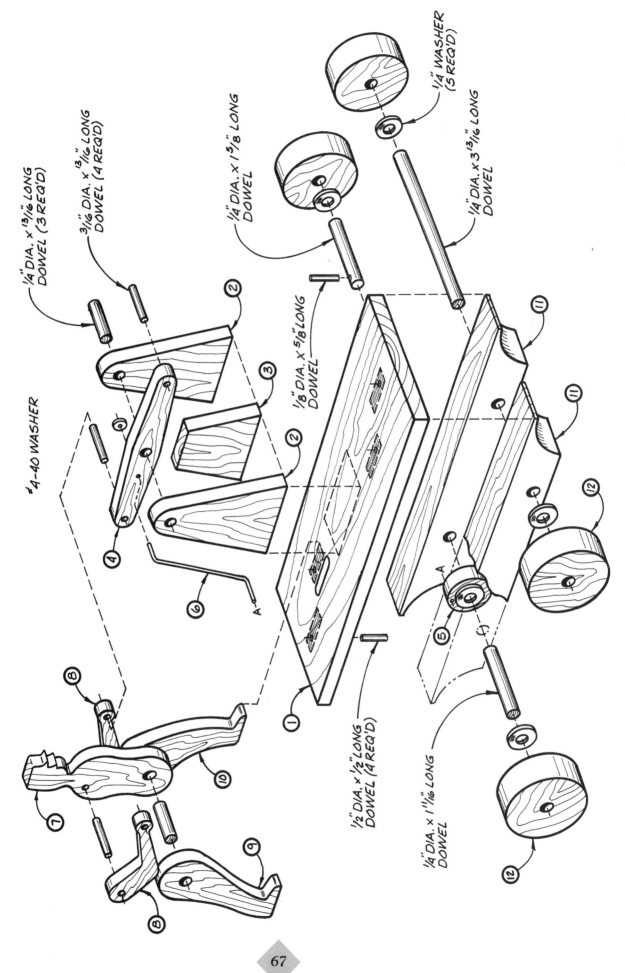

¼" DIA. x ¹³/₁₆" LONG DOWEL (3 REQ'D)

³/₁₆" DIA. x ¹³/₁₆" LONG DOWEL (4 REQ'D)

¼" DIA. x 1⁵/₈" LONG DOWEL

¼" WASHER (5 REQ'D)

¼" DIA. x 3¹³/₁₆" LONG DOWEL

⅛" DIA. x ⅝" LONG DOWEL

#4-40 WASHER

½" DIA. x ½" LONG DOWEL (4 REQ'D)

¼" DIA. x 1¹¹/₁₆" LONG DOWEL

HAND-POWERED RAILCAR
FULL-SIZE PATTERNS

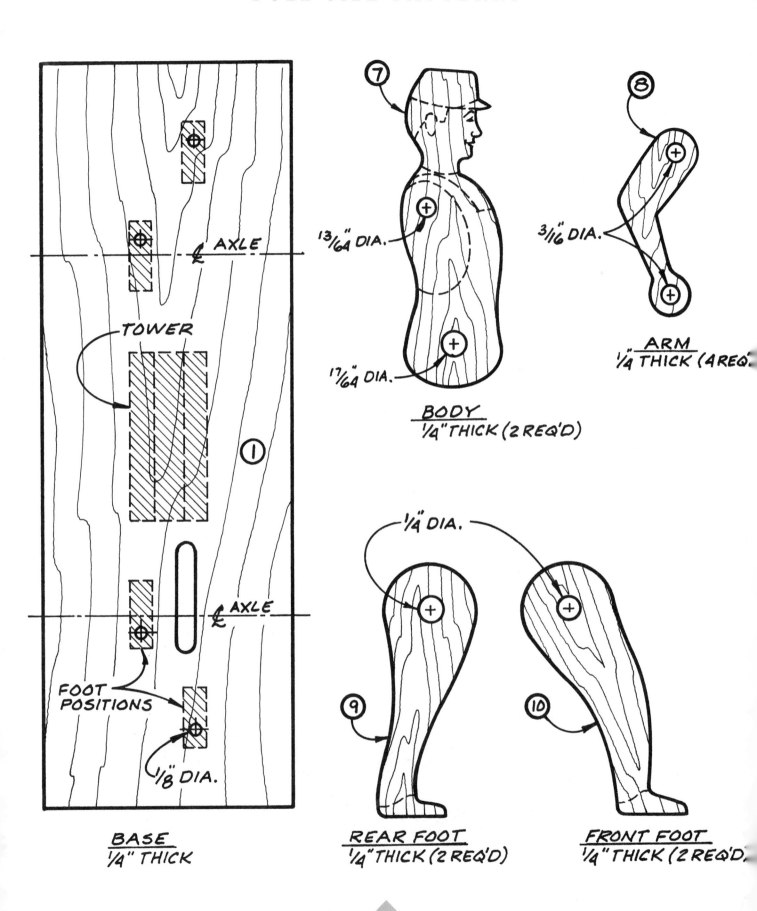

AXLE

TOWER

①

FOOT POSITIONS

1/8" DIA.

BASE
1/4" THICK

AXLE

⑦

13/64" DIA.

17/64" DIA.

BODY
1/4" THICK (2 REQ'D)

⑧

3/16" DIA.

ARM
1/4 THICK (4 REQ'D)

1/4" DIA.

⑨

REAR FOOT
1/4" THICK (2 REQ'D)

⑩

FRONT FOOT
1/4" THICK (2 REQ'D)

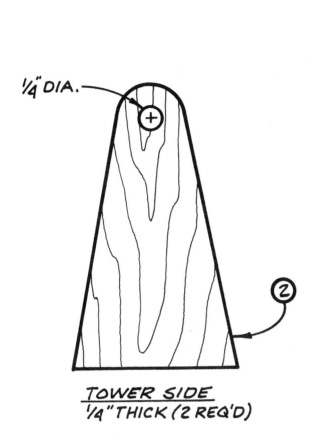

1/4" DIA.

②

TOWER SIDE
1/4" THICK (2 REQ'D)

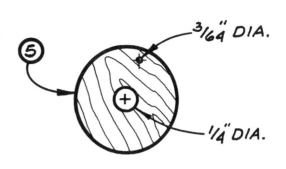

⑤

3/64" DIA.

1/4" DIA.

DRIVE DISK
1/4" THICK

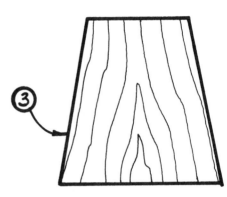

③

TOWER CENTER
5/16" THICK

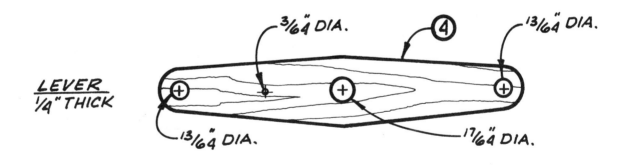

3/64" DIA.

④

13/64" DIA.

LEVER
1/4" THICK

13/64" DIA.

17/64" DIA.

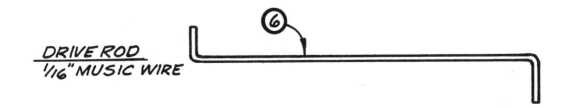

⑥

DRIVE ROD
1/16" MUSIC WIRE

HINGED DACHSHUND

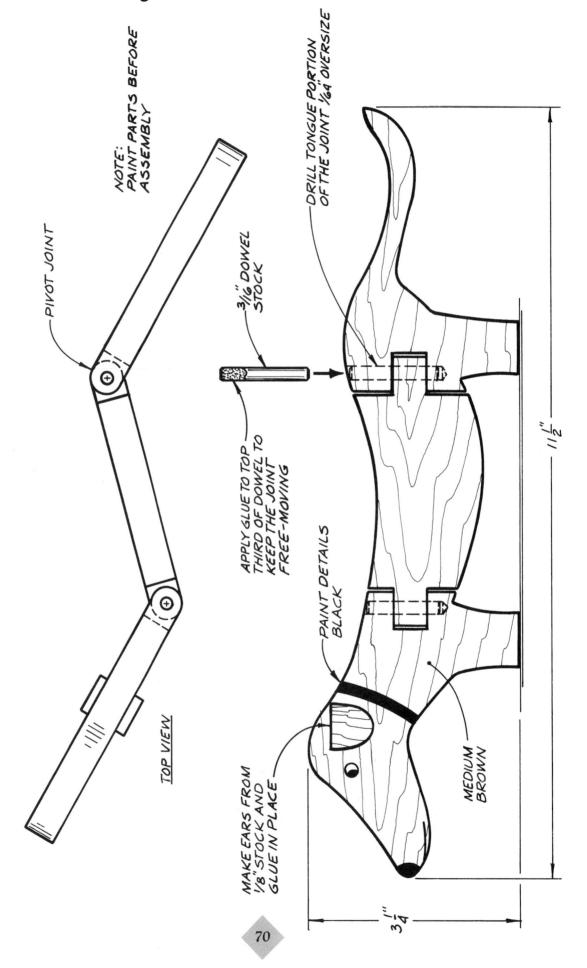

NOTE:
PAINT PARTS BEFORE
ASSEMBLY

PIVOT JOINT

DRILL TONGUE PORTION
OF THE JOINT 1/64 OVERSIZE

3/16" DOWEL
STOCK

APPLY GLUE TO TOP
THIRD OF DOWEL TO
KEEP THE JOINT
FREE-MOVING

PAINT DETAILS
BLACK

MEDIUM
BROWN

TOP VIEW

MAKE EARS FROM
1/8" STOCK AND
GLUE IN PLACE

11 1/2"

3 1/4"

FULL-SIZE PATTERNS

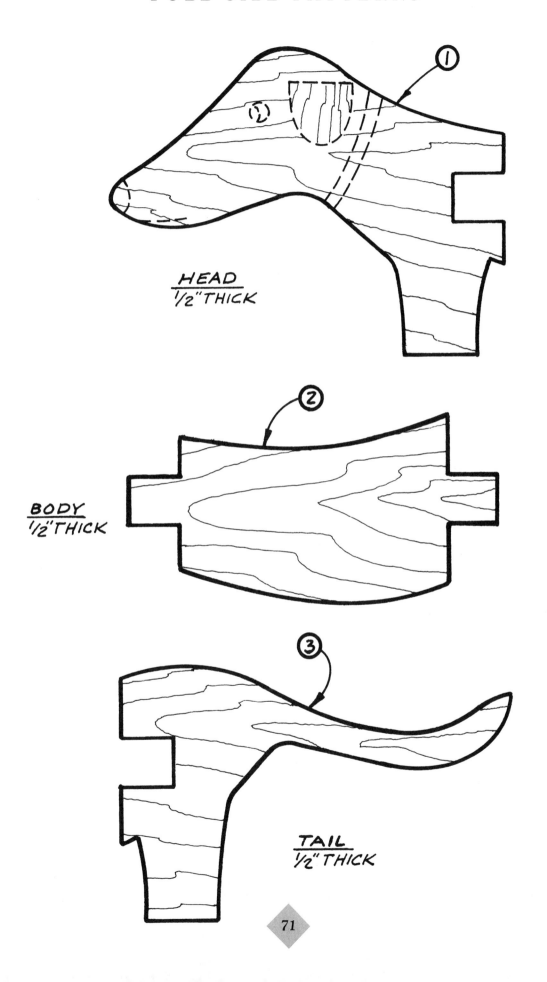

HEAD
1/2"THICK

BODY
1/2"THICK

TAIL
1/2"THICK

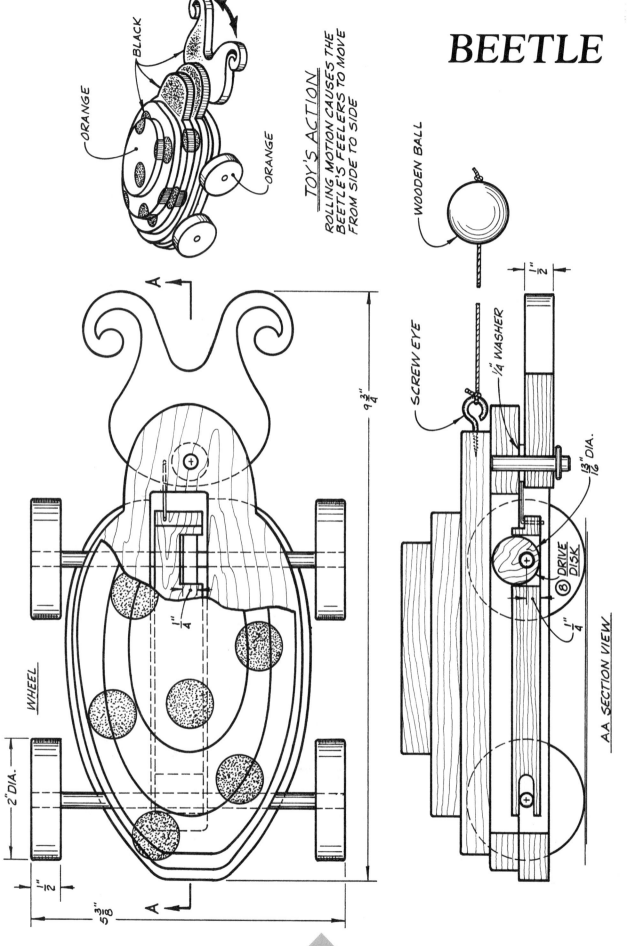

BEETLE

BLACK

ORANGE

ORANGE

TOY'S ACTION
ROLLING MOTION CAUSES THE
BEETLE'S FEELERS TO MOVE
FROM SIDE TO SIDE

WOODEN BALL

SCREW EYE

¼ WASHER

$\frac{13}{16}$" DIA.

DRIVE
⑧ DISK

$\frac{1}{4}$"

$\frac{1}{2}$"

AA SECTION VIEW

WHEEL

2" DIA.

$\frac{1}{4}$"

$9\frac{3}{4}$"

$\frac{1}{2}$"

$5\frac{3}{8}$"

A

A

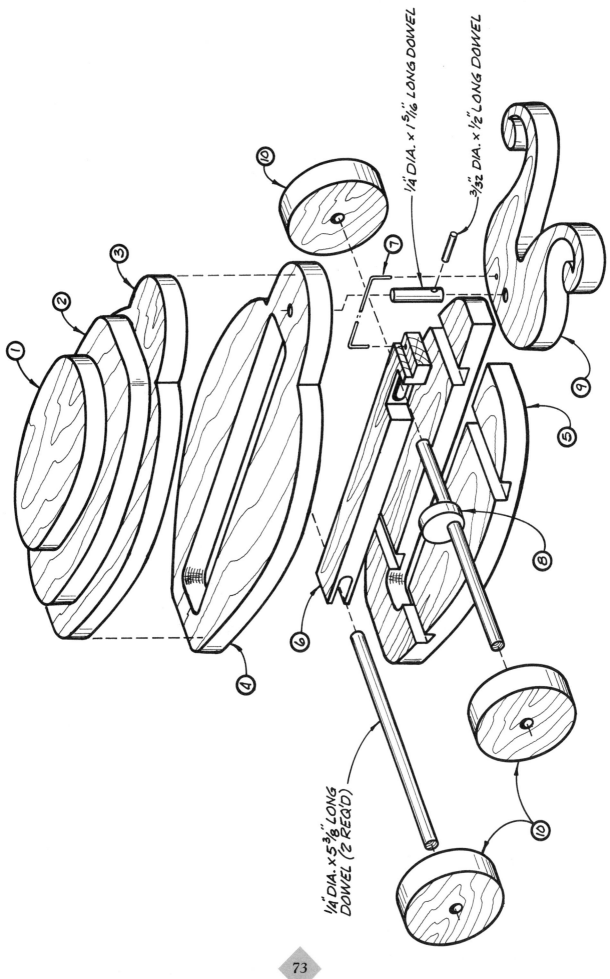

¼" DIA. × 1 5/16" LONG DOWEL

3/32" DIA. × ½ LONG DOWEL

¼" DIA. × 5 3/8" LONG DOWEL (2 REQ'D)

BEETLE
FULL-SIZE PATTERNS

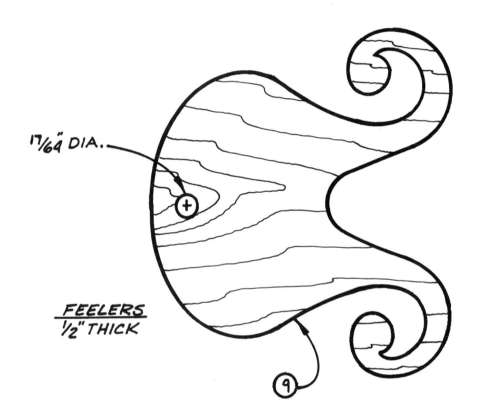

17/64" DIA.

+

FEELERS
1/2" THICK

9

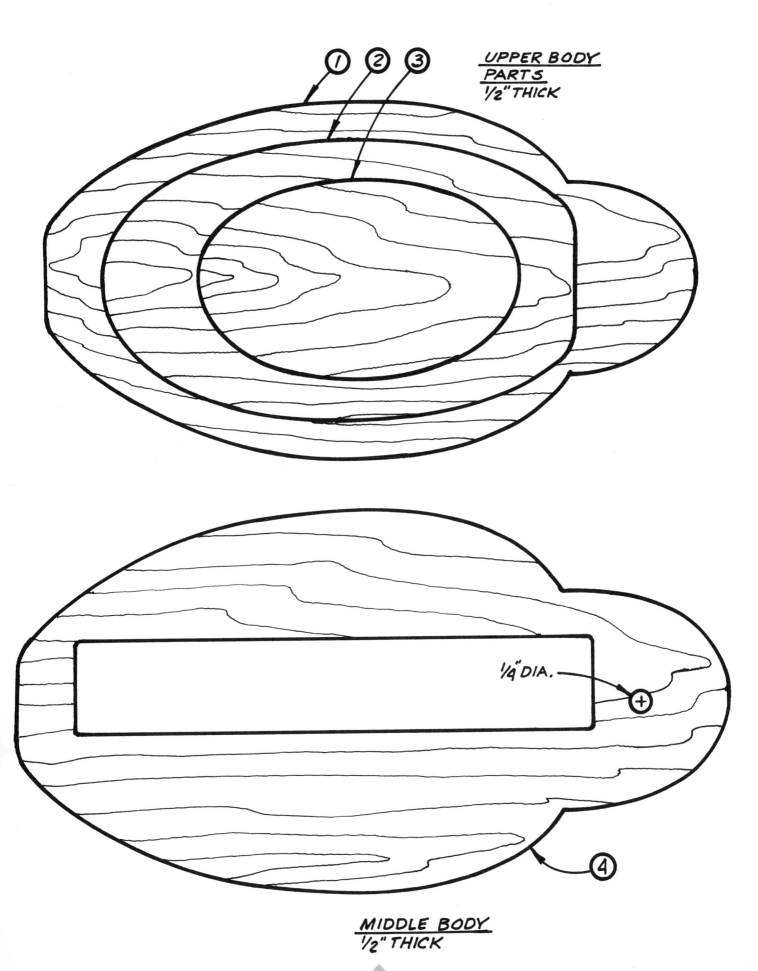

① ② ③

UPPER BODY
PARTS
1/2" THICK

1/4" DIA.

+

④

MIDDLE BODY
1/2" THICK

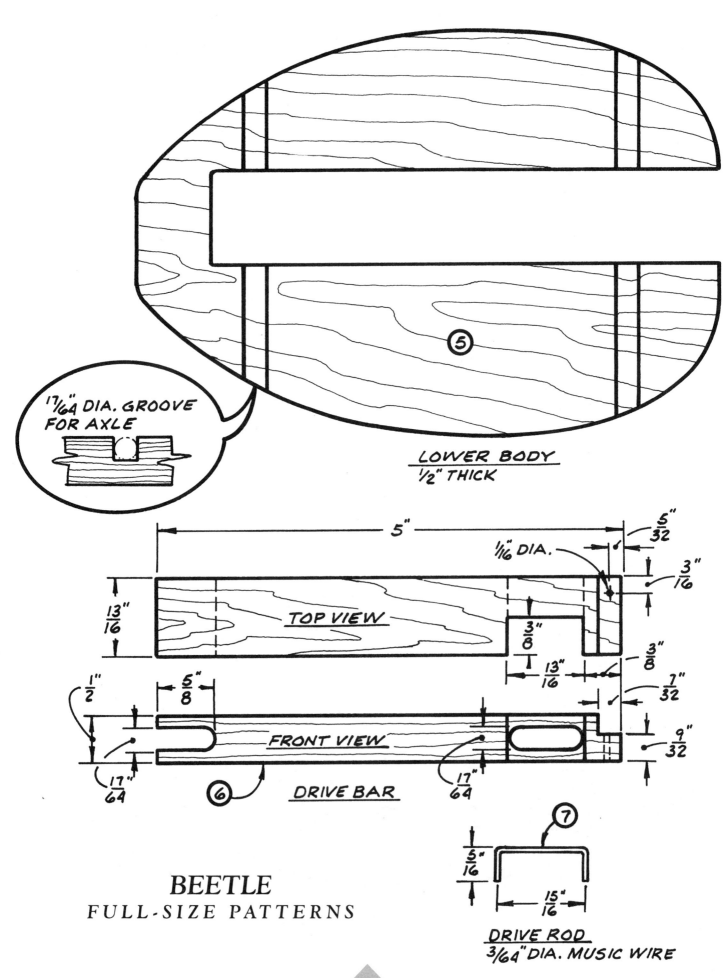

¹⁷⁄₆₄" DIA. GROOVE FOR AXLE

⑤

LOWER BODY
½" THICK

5"

⁵⁄₃₂"

¹⁄₁₆ DIA.

³⁄₁₆

¹³⁄₁₆"

TOP VIEW

³⁄₈"

³⁄₈"

¹³⁄₁₆"

⁷⁄₃₂"

¹⁄₂"

⁵⁄₈"

FRONT VIEW

⑥

¹⁷⁄₆₄"

DRIVE BAR

¹⁷⁄₆₄"

⁹⁄₃₂"

⑦

⁵⁄₁₆"

¹⁵⁄₁₆"

DRIVE ROD
³⁄₆₄" DIA. MUSIC WIRE

BEETLE
FULL-SIZE PATTERNS

Sources of Supply

The following list of suppliers can be used to help find the materials, hardware, and tools for your projects. Each company provides a mail-order service and catalog or price list for its products.

Dick Blick Art Materials
PO Box 26
Allentown, PA 18105
(800) 933-2542

Certainly Wood
11753 Big Tree Rd.
RR 20A
East Aurora, NY 14052
(716) 655-0206

Cherry Tree Toys
PO Box 369
Belmont, OH 43718
(800) 848-4363

Albert Constantine and Son, Inc.
2050 Eastchester Rd.
Bronx, NY 10461
(800) 223-8087

House of Tools
100 Mayfield Common NW
102 Ave. and Mayfield Rd.
Edmonton, AB T5P4K9
Canada
(800) 661-3987

Lee Valley Tools
PO Box 1780
Ogdensburg, NY 13669-6780
(800) 267-8735

Manny's Woodworker's Place
555 S Broadway
Lexington, KY 40508
(800) 243-0713

Treeline
1305 E 1120 S
Provo, UT 84606
(800) 598-2743

Trend-lines
135 American Legion Highway
Revere, MA 02151
(800) 767-9999

Steve Wall Lumber Co.
PO Box 287
Mayodan, NC 27027
(800) 633-4062

Wildwood Designs, Inc.
PO Box 676
Richland Center, WI 53581
(800) 470-9090

Woodcraft Supply
PO Box 1686
Parkersburg, WV 26102-1686
(800) 535-4482

Woodcrafter's Lumber Sales
212 NE 6th Ave.
Portland, OR 97232-2976
(800) 777-3709

The Woodworkers' Store
4365 Willow Dr.
Medina, MN 55340-9701
(800) 279-4441

Woodworker's Supply
5604 Alameda Place NE
Albuquerque, NM 87113
(800) 645-9292

Metric Conversions

INCHES TO MILLIMETERS

IN.	MM	IN.	MM
1	25.4	51	1295.4
2	50.8	52	1320.8
3	76.2	53	1346.2
4	101.6	54	1371.6
5	127.0	55	1397.0
6	152.4	56	1422.4
7	177.8	57	1447.8
8	203.2	58	1473.2
9	228.6	59	1498.6
10	254.0	60	1524.0
11	279.4	61	1549.4
12	304.8	62	1574.8
13	330.2	63	1600.2
14	355.6	64	1625.6
15	381.0	65	1651.0
16	406.4	66	1676.4
17	431.8	67	1701.8
18	457.2	68	1727.2
19	482.6	69	1752.6
20	508.0	70	1778.0
21	533.4	71	1803.4
22	558.8	72	1828.8
23	584.2	73	1854.2
24	609.6	74	1879.6
25	635.0	75	1905.0
26	660.4	76	1930.4
27	685.8	77	1955.8
28	711.2	78	1981.2
29	736.6	79	2006.6
30	762.0	80	2032.0
31	787.4	81	2057.4
32	812.8	82	2082.8
33	838.2	83	2108.2
34	863.6	84	2133.6
35	889.0	85	2159.0
36	914.4	86	2184.4
37	939.8	87	2209.8
38	965.2	88	2235.2
39	990.6	89	2260.6
40	1016.0	90	2286.0
41	1041.4	91	2311.4
42	1066.8	92	2336.8
43	1092.2	93	2362.2
44	1117.6	94	2387.6
45	1143.0	95	2413.0
46	1168.4	96	2438.4
47	1193.8	97	2463.8
48	1219.2	98	2489.2
49	1244.6	99	2514.6
50	1270.0	100	2540.0

The above table is exact on the basis: 1 in. = 25.4 mm

U.S. TO METRIC

1 inch	=	2.540 centimeters
1 foot	=	.305 meter
1 yard	=	.914 meter
1 mile	=	1.609 kilometers

METRIC TO U.S.

1 millimeter	=	.039 inch
1 centimeter	=	.394 inch
1 meter	=	3.281 feet or 1.094 yards
1 kilometer	=	.621 mile

INCH-METRIC EQUIVALENTS

Fraction	Decimal Equivalent Customary (IN.)	Metric (MM)	Fraction	Decimal Equivalent Customary (IN.)	Metric (MM)
1/64	.015	0.3969	33/64	.515	13.0969
1/32	.031	0.7938	17/32	.531	13.4938
3/64	.046	1.1906	35/64	.546	13.8906
1/16	.062	1.5875	9/16	.562	14.2875
5/64	.078	1.9844	37/64	.578	14.6844
3/32	.093	2.3813	19/32	.593	15.0813
7/64	.109	2.7781	39/64	.609	15.4781
1/8	.125	3.1750	5/8	.625	15.8750
9/64	.140	3.5719	41/64	.640	16.2719
5/32	.156	3.9688	21/32	.656	16.6688
11/64	.171	4.3656	43/64	.671	17.0656
3/16	.187	4.7625	11/16	.687	17.4625
13/64	.203	5.1594	45/64	.703	17.8594
7/32	.218	5.5563	23/32	.718	18.2563
15/64	.234	5.9531	47/64	.734	18.6531
1/4	.250	6.3500	3/4	.750	19.0500
17/64	.265	6.7469	49/64	.765	19.4469
9/32	.281	7.1438	25/32	.781	19.8438
19/64	.296	7.5406	51/64	.796	20.2406
5/16	.312	7.9375	13/16	.812	20.6375
21/64	.328	8.3384	53/64	.828	21.0344
11/32	.343	8.7313	27/32	.843	21.4313
23/64	.359	9.1281	55/64	.859	21.8281
3/8	.375	9.5250	7/8	.875	22.2250
25/64	.390	9.9219	57/64	.890	22.6219
13/32	.406	10.3188	29/32	.906	23.0188
27/64	.421	10.7156	59/64	.921	23.4156
7/16	.437	11.1125	15/16	.937	23.8125
29/64	.453	11.5094	61/64	.953	24.2094
15/32	.468	11.9063	31/32	.968	24.6063
31/64	.484	12.3031	63/64	.984	25.0031
1/2	.500	12.7000	1	1.000	25.4000

For additional patterns,
try these other scroll saw books from Stackpole . . .

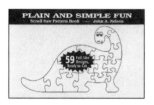